A Chiltern Hundred

by Keith Bosley

poems
THE POSSIBILITY OF ANGELS (1969)
THE THREE HOUSES (1976)
DARK SUMMER (1976)
STATIONS (1979)

translations
RUSSIA'S OTHER POETS (1968)
AN IDIOM OF NIGHT: PIERRE JEAN JOUVE (1968)
THE WAR WIFE: VIETNAMESE POETRY (1972)
THE SONG OF AINO, FROM THE KALEVALA (1973)
THE SONG OF SONGS (1976)
FINNISH FOLK POETRY: EPIC (1977)
MALLARMÉ: THE POEMS (1977)
A ROUND O: ANDRÉ FRÉNAUD (1977)
THE LAST TEMPTATIONS: OPERA BY JOONAS KOKKONEN (1977)
WHITSONGS: EINO LEINO (1978)
THE ELEK BOOK OF ORIENTAL VERSE (1979)
A READING OF ASHES: JERZY FICOWSKI (1981)
FROM THE THEOREMS OF MASTER JEAN DE LA CEPPÈDE (1983)
WANTON LOVERBOY, FROM THE KALEVALA (1985)

for children
TALES FROM THE LONG LAKES: FINNISH LEGENDS (1966)
AND I DANCE (1972)

Keith Bosley

A CHILTERN HUNDRED

Anvil Press Poetry

Published in 1987
by Anvil Press Poetry Ltd
69 King George Street London SE10 8PX
and 27 South Main Street Wolfeboro NH 03894 USA

Copyright © Keith Bosley 1987

This book is published
with financial assistance from
The Arts Council of Great Britain

Set in Joanna
by Bryan Williamson, Manchester
Printed and bound in England
at The Camelot Press, Southampton

British Library Cataloguing in Publication Data

Bosley, Keith
   A Chiltern hundred.
   I. Title
   821'.914   PR6052.O73

   ISBN 0-85646-175-X
   ISBN 0-85646-176-8 Pbk

Library of Congress Cataloging-in-Publication Data

Bosley, Keith.
   A Chiltern hundred.

   I. Title.
PR6052.O73C48   1986   821'.914   86-3480

in memory of
MAXWELL FRASER

ACKNOWLEDGEMENTS

to the editors of the following journals in which many of these poems first appeared: *Agenda, Books, Country Life, Fountains* (Marseilles), *Kudos, Langley Parish Magazine, New Statesman, Outposts, Poésie 1* (Paris), *Poetry Review, The Times Literary Supplement, Wheels*. One poem appeared in *Ma'ariv* (Jerusalem) in a Hebrew translation by Moshe Dor. Two poems were broadcast by BBC Radio 3 in 'Poetry Now'. Some poems first appeared in *New Poetry 2* and *New Poetry 3* (The Arts Council of Great Britain) and in *A Fourth Poetry Book* (Oxford University Press). 'Slough Station: Broad Gauge' won a prize in a competition sponsored in 1976 by *The Daily Telegraph Magazine* for the Cheltenham Literature Festival, and was printed in the *Telegraph Sunday Magazine*. The sonnets won a prize as a sequence in the Arvon Foundation Poetry Competition 1980 in association with 'The South Bank Show', London Weekend Television, and were printed in the Foundation's 1980 *Anthology* (Kilnhurst Publishing Company).

Contents

1	HOME TOWN	11
2	MOAT AT CIPPENHAM	13
3	THE CHALVEY STABMONK	14
4	THE UPTON YEW	15
5	CONVERGENCE	16
6	CHALVEY CHURCH	18
7	MEMORIAL	19
8	ELEGY FOR MACKENZIE STREET	20
9	FAMOUS RESIDENT	21
10	BLACKLEAD CASTLE	22
11	MINSTREL	23
12	Dipping my langue de chat	25
13	REVERSION AT COLNBROOK	26
14	POCOCK'S LANE	27
15	WORDS AGAINST THE NIGHT	31
16	PETITION	32
17	UPTON PARK	34
18	ON A THEME OF JAMES JOYCE	35
19	THE CHIMNEY	36
20	SAGA	37
21	WATERS ABOVE	39
22	Knowing the desert places	40
23	SLOUGH STATION: BROAD GAUGE	41
24	AT DATCHET STATION	42
25	DEPARTURE	43
26	ULYSSES	44
27	DORIS	45
28	ALPHA STREET	47
29	THE BRUSH	49
30	THE WRITING ON THE WALL	50
31	ARSON	51
32	THE POTTER'S FIELD	52
33	CORPUS CHRISTI	54
34	You mention my canal	55

35	MR HOLMES	56
36	SEED MERCHANT	57
37	MARKET	58
38	PASTORAL	60
39	TO TAKE AWAY	61
40	MR GUNN	62
41	TRADESMEN	63
42	LAST SPRING	64
43	CAT AND SICK CHILD	65
44	AN IRISHWOMAN VISITS HER SON	66
45	MAN OF LETTERS	68
46	*Listen, this town*	69
47	IN MEMORY OF SID OSBORNE	70
48	GENERAL PRACTITIONER	71
49	LULU	72
50	THE BOGOMILS	73
51	THE WEDDING GUEST	74
52	*We have discussed the Seven Trances*	82
53	SISTER	83
54	SHARED CHURCH	84
55	PERIOD WEDDING	85
56	GIPSY FUNERAL	87
57	HYMN TUNE PRELUDE	88
58	TWO MINUTES' SILENCE	89
59	KNELL, MINOR, DOUBLES [-61]	90
62	*I watch the ringers*	93
63	PROCESSION	94
64	INCIDENT AT ETON	95
65	MUSICAL RIDE	96
66	HOLY SATURDAY	97
67	SATURDAY NIGHT	98
68	ASSUMPTION	99
69	LIMBO DANCE	101
70	PALMY DAYS	103
71	ROMNEY	105
72	A PRIVATE PERSON	108
73	*So intimate, the poet says*	110
74	FOR JOHN PHILLIPS [-77]	111

78	FOR PHILIP BERGNER [-84]	113
85	*It is your hour*	118
86	CECILIA NEAL [-91]	119
92	RESURRECTION	126
93	*All Saints*	130
94	SUNNYMEADS	131
95	ENCOUNTER	135
96	THE WHITE PEACOCK	136
97	THE ELDERBERRY TREE	137
98	TRACKS	138
99	*When you are old*	139
100	MOVING INDOORS	140
	NOTES	142

1

Home Town

Before the blooms, the bricks, the embrocation
there were the chalk hills, the clay terraces
the waters dwindling to the name of Thames:
here people hunted, planted, dug a moat
raised a mound by a brook that runs through fields
to a fair grove of willows: yesterday
this was a village, Chalvey, where each Whitsun
a plaster beast was buried, a mock mayor
was made, baptised and robed in someone's curtains –
a lawless place where policemen walked in pairs.
But luckier poor men's sons sent up the cry
Ad montem! in their new tongue, crossed the fields
from Eton College to play highwaymen
in Turkish caftans with a jingling band
to demand salt-money, *salarium*
of the rich where the Bath Road climbs Salt Hill.
Eastward and off the road, the Merton Priors
built Upton church of the Ivy-mantled Tow'r –
Norman on Saxon ruins, ruined in turn:
behind it Upton Court was old when James
leased it to Robert Barker, Printer to
the Kings Most Excellent Maiestie of his Bible.
Northward, a marshy hamlet where Brunel
built a Great Western Railway station, called it
after the hamlet Slough.
                        Upton-cum-Chalvey
is still the name on parish notice boards:
no brickfields, but some nurseries remain
and orchards where they still remember Cox
brewer, retired, of Colnbrook with his pippin –
and factories, a great brow to the north
curving from the canal west to the Dump
for army lorries from the First World War.
A vision here, the first trading estate –

a railway line serving each factory
and flowerbeds, lawns, canteens, a community centre.
A vision too a hundred years before
when Herschel held a prism to the sun
and wondered why the red rays on his face
felt warmer. Arago was lyrical:
Le nom de ce village ne périra jamais.
A town untried by tourists, handy for
London and yet apart from it, somewhere
for refugees from want or tyranny
to start afresh in Alpha Street and beyond –
terrace on terrace reaching to the Chilterns
where prep schools, swimming pools and golf clubs rule.
Plenty of body, little soul: it needed
tons of hardcore, and still you cannot build
heavy or high. Remember that if you
take it into your head to write it down.

2
Moat at Cippenham

Someone with a Celtic name · built his hall
    hereabouts before Rome
  made inroads or ton and ham
  and ley staked out a kingdom.

He dug a moat and within · the earth-ring
    he thronged with all his kin
  but long silent is the din
  of men, women and children.

Even the ploughman who swore · at this creased
    acre is here no more
  and the cattle do not care
  how crooked is their pasture.

Even these words though they dance · to a tune
    noted centuries since
  have no vowels and consonants
  to echo such a distance.

No ghosts, or they are misheard · like Herne the
    Hunter who had in ward
  the deer of his Tudor lord
  but was once a god, antlered.

The place is empty and yet · so man-filled
    I feel I ought to quit
  and I fall over my feet
  as if I have been thrown out.

3

The Chalvey Stabmonk

They told me it was a monkey
an organ grinder's beast
but I wondered why each Whitsun
they honoured it with a feast.

They told me it was begging
in their poor village street
but I wondered why its thick tail rose
erect between its feet.

They told me it bit an urchin
whose father stabbed it dead
but I wondered why its hollow eyes
stared out of its domed head.

They told me how for pity
they gave it a funeral
but I wondered why its mourners were
baptised and robed and all.

They told me how their grandads
had made this plaster cast
but I wondered why their monkey
must be rebuilt to last.

For this is Chalvey, Calf Island
with healing well and mound
which for all those centuries
were reckoned holy ground.

I told them there was more to that
Stabmonk than meets the eye
but all they did was tell me to
go forth and multiply.

4
The Upton Yew

Before the puddingstones were laid
and the round chancel roof was raised
the yew was there, guarding its dead
and gods of earth and air were praised.

A thousand years, knowing no foe
it wrestled with itself, played both
striker and stricken in a slow
agony of luxuriant growth.

But while its limbs became longbows
the rain found out a tender part
in its trunk, secret as a rose
and buried arrows in its heart.

Yet still it thickened – sixteen feet
it measured round – until the wind
took it by storm last night and split
what centuries could never bend.

Now its true colours are revealed:
decay has never looked so rich
and the church folk, the time fulfilled
are going to burn it like a witch.

5

Convergence

'On 15 June I went from Windsor
to' (here a blank space) 'to Dr Herschel
where I saw the great telescope.'
         1792:
Herr Kapellmeister Haydn on his first
trip to England, the concert season over
went west to Windsor, stood upon the Terrace
and called the view divine, descended thence
northward across the Thames, through the college
the playing-fields of Eton, to the hamlet
whose name he did not catch – some coaching-inns
along the Great Bath Road, a farm, a ruined
church whose ivy-mantled tower a poet
had lately praised.
     Here planetary man
Herr Doktor with the stars about his head
had settled after finding Uranus
to wonder why the red end of the spectrum
was warmer than the violet, to wed
a local widow, set up house and raise
a family – indoors a son, outside
on the front lawn a tangle of ladders, masts
from which a mighty tube reared like a cannon
heavenward: *coelorum perrupit claustra*
it says now on his tomb.
       Haydn took down
the measurements – forty feet by five: here was
a fellow German from the busy North
who had come to England as a young musician –
and was not Handel master of them both?
But where the quick South had turned from fugue
to symphony, this Northerner had turned
to the heavens, grinding his own lenses
sitting out in the deepest, sharpest winter
calling down constellations, nebulas

into the known sphere.
                        Past sixty now
his good Prince gone, this Southerner must follow
in the master's footsteps, but first must ask
a question of this man who had seen further
than any man before, this visionary:
'Is it true, Herr Doktor, that the world
was created in six days?'
                        The reply
was roundabout: there was light, yes, but light
in turbulence, millions of wheeling points
our earth, indeed our sun with many earths
but one of them.
                        So the astronomer
told the musician what the heavens told him –
the glory of God, set down in chart and table:
there was still time to turn it back to man –
the key C minor, two beats to the bar.

6
Chalvey Church

> *We the people of Chalvey*
> *do wish that there should*
> *be A small Church erected*
> *As our little place is so small*
> *that it do not afford sufficient*
> *room for our congregation and*
> *we are A trying to lay the*
> *foundation of A new one we*
> *are putting in our mite and we*
> *hope God will bless our undertaking*
> *although A very humble one.*

A scrap of paper framed in the village church
the document inscribed in a horny hand
    is dated 1855 and
  signed on behalf of the persons present.

Set down beside each name (there are thirty-three)
the sum contributed: it is thirty-one
    shillings in all, one tithe apiece, the
  price of a novel if they could read it.

The hand is David Brill's, with a shilling paid
and after six years, after Her Majesty
    stumped up a hundred pounds (His local
  Grace followed suit for *noblesse* obliged him)

this David Brill as verger was leading an
episcopal procession to consecrate
    St Peter's. In stained glass he looks with
  Simeon's eyes that have seen salvation.

7

Memorial

for Anthony Rudolf

> James Elliman, son
> of embrocation
> to commemorate
> his kin took the west
> window of Slough church

but being a man

who cared for bodies

not souls he wanted

no saints no haloes

which was a problem

till he heard about

Modern Art and met

Alfred A. Wolmark

Jewish refugee

from Christian Poland

who completed me

in 1917:

zealously shunning

image and likeness

my four tall panes tipped

with what otherwise

would have been a star

refract at evening

through their mosaic

purple orange green

the Shekinah wink

at the priest as he

turns west and intones

the benediction.

8

Elegy for Mackenzie Street

for Colin and Mary Shepherdson

Where is the street which once connected the town to the
    station
  joining railway to road, wedding the new with the old?
Here was a village of inns, and then Brunel with his iron
  hammered the way of his will, west, parallel to the road
raised a magnificent roof where his copper-caparisoned
    horses
  feeding on water and coal, waited for passengers – yes
Queen Victoria too, in the Royal Hotel by the station
  taking her ease in a chair borne from the halls of Versailles
and admiring the work of Monsieur Gobelin's weavers
  till Brunel's royal line forged on to Windsor and home.
Ruin befell the hotel, but now one Major Mackenzie
  visited leafy Slough, bought and improved the estate
made it over in trust to the British Orphan Asylum
  and the hotel was rebuilt opposite, next to the mews.
They are no more, but the spot still rings with the chatter
    of children
  wearing a uniform too – that of a fee-paying school.
Up from the station, flanked by hotel and what was asylum
  ran that street which was named after the merciful man:
broadly it ran and fair, with tall and prosperous houses
  hidden in spring by trees' orderly riots of bloom
forming a long slow curve from the station up to the High
    Street
  making the whole one town, elegant, all of a piece.
Now with the motor car and with the ring road comes the
    deception:
  railways cut into land, they do not cut into lives –
that is for tarmac to do. For the town has shifted its centre
  and, under siege by road, now it is sitting awry.
All those houses are down and the curve is lost in the
    concrete.
  Gone is Mackenzie Street, but for a place to reverse.

9
Famous Resident

Dickens lived here, but no memorial plaque
outside this supermarket says so: here
a cottage once was, here
his Nelly turned those last, bitterest years
to a brief sweetness.
                        But the world said no –
would have said no, if it had had the chance
for old Boz covered up his tracks so well
no one is certain even now. A page
in a cheap diary drops the clues – train times
place names pared down to initials: add a few
doubtful entries in rate books, registers –
it all adds up. Too many innocents
depended on him in that lily world
with Rochester come back as Cloisterham
ready to black him still.
                          A hundred years
pass, and his village is a town: I walk
behind the supermarket down a dark
alley he would have known
and hear on the bright street this spring evening
today's citizens shout, knowing their rights.

10

Blacklead Castle

Blacklead Castle the name top-hatted neighbours called
this brick folly with towers, pinnacles, battlements
    lancets, mock-Gothic windows
  sanctimoniously adorned

dreamed and built by a man richer than they, who mined
graphite, marketed it, called it The Servants' Friend
    and Victorian households
  blacked their fenders and made his pile.

Blacklead Castle today still is a dream of home
but for daughters and sons grown in their season old
    of those lives that were ruled by
  wiping on and by brushing off

dozing slumped in the State their benefactor's house
letting somebody else just for a change get on
    with the sweeping of floors, the
  chores, the dusting of furniture

while their tea trolley comes loaded with little cups
bread and butter and jam, napkins in napkin rings
    and they graciously sip and
  dip as though to the manner born.

Moulded ceilings resound when a tin tray is dropped
handrails gleam everywhere, screwed into coats-of-arms:
    Blacklead Castle has fallen –
  fallen into the rightful hands.

11

Minstrel

    Just out of town
life has always moved
slowly – the gravestone
with UNDERNEATH carved

    in capitals
larger than the name
for comfort, the scowls
that if asked proclaim

    this village's
loyalty to the
King three centuries
ago, the oak tree

    on the green where
a man in a wide-
brimmed hat spoke thunder
against the slave trade:

    under the same
tree today a man
sits down. Where he came
from no gossip can

    hazard a guess:
not in overalls
but in morning dress
trim from head to heels

    lacking only
a straw hat and cane
he flexes a knee
crosses his legs, then

    he starts talking
and waving his hands
on which a gold ring
winks. A small boy stands

    nearby, listens
then shrugs his shoulders
as small boys do, runs
off with shouts of 'Here's

    a nut-case!' to
his friends up the road.
Now the man has no
audience: his flood

    of rhetoric
is however not
stemmed, nor are his quick
gestures any jot

    retarded. Small
boys diagnose bats
in belfries with cool
skill: cruelty? That's

    our affair. One
glance from a Negro
(say it with caution
for he bites, you know)

    and he is to
blame for greenfly, bad
harvests, riots: no
wonder he is mad.

12

Dipping my langue de chat in a cup of tea
and then spooning it out, I leave to Proust
the labour of redeeming all that past
and think about the present – you and me.

Langue de chat – yes, a biscuit, but also
the language of your cat which understands
what only you say to it as your hands
close round it in a way I do not know.

But there are other languages: I study
the delicate declensions of your body
whose conjugations wed me to despair

for to you I am neither noun nor verb
and when my spittle, sweat or tears disturb
catlike you shake my moisture from your hair.

13

Reversion at Colnbrook

Quite the grandest house that was not a coaching
inn, yet somehow grim in its workhouse brick – bay
windows looking out on a well kept garden
        blazing with roses

which have all returned to the wild and grass grows
high where there was once a herbaceous border:
people leave this village in droves because of
        noise from the airport

but this lady left for the oldest reason
and this host of cars in the driveway means that
soon her house and all its effects are coming
        under the hammer.

Strangers' feet are soiling the once scrubbed doorstep
dropping mud and marching from hall to parlour
upstairs, downstairs, tramping from room to room, eyes
        peering at corners:

every chair and table and bed and cupboard
has been numbered, crockery and utensils
too, and knives, forks, spoons are arranged like scalpels
        for a post mortem.

This small bookcase offers *The Leisure Hour*, Sir
Walter Scott and Dickens in mint condition
Huntingtower, *Black Beauty*, the Bible and *The*
        Methodist Hymn Book.

Pictures? Not so much as a pale rectangle
but one text: MY KINGDOM IS NOT OF THIS WORLD
Yet the locals say that the old girl owned a
        third of the village.

14

Pocock's Lane

>for Ben Bosley

'Where's Pocock's Lane?' the lorry driver calls
from his high cab. Behind him fifteen tons
shudders, sighs to a halt, and the air fills
with diesel fumes. But little else remains

of Pocock, John, owner of Willowbrook
and Upton farms and all adjoining lands
one of the richest men in all this Stoke
Hundred, but pious, giving fifty pounds

to save old Upton church from demolition:
lightning had struck the Ivy-mantled Tow'r
and the whole fabric was in poor condition.
As nearby Eton struck the curfew hour

Thomas Gray lately walked from fair Stoke Poges
and called the churchyard a neglected Spot:
now it was time to think of coming ages
to rescue Herschel's tomb and stop the rot.

This Eton Road with cool Victorian villas
a little school, a house of prayer, becomes
the lane named after Pocock where the willows
of Agars Plough bend it to touch the Thames.

Ben, my son, on our tandem we would spin
this way through Eton, cross the main street, go
to Dorney: BEST KEPT VILLAGE says a sign
and opposite another sign says SLOW.

Here a Victorian pub, a Georgian shop
a Jacobean cottage on whose roof
doves cluster. In the garden, pumps: you stop
for petrol, pass the time of day, drive off

admiring not a leaf, a bloom, a sash
a curtain out of place from one end where
a lady walks a poodle on a leash
and gentlemen in plus fours take the air

and an intrepid band of tourists seeks
among the trees the Court's wrought iron gates
to the other where the schoolhouse sells antiques
its windows full of little pale round plates.

But back into Stoke Hundred: leave the village
rumbling across the cattle grid and out
on to the windy common: castle, college
Boveney, river boats over to the right

and to the left, beyond the motorway
and railway, rise the cooling towers, the pylons
out of Slough's humming mass of industry
though this far from it all is steam and silence.

And silence once across the cattle grid
in the next village, silence at its heart
behind the noisy council house façade –
not peace but silence: keep the two apart.

A house, a stream, a farm, but not a soul.
The rooks have vanished since the elms were felled
but other birds and other trees as well
as though the Belle Dame Sans Merci had called.

A dream, factories in the countryside
becomes a nightmare when industrial waste
is used for fertiliser, purified
but not enough: the marriage was in haste

for chemicals that kill bacteria
and knock the wicked microbe on the head
are useful creatures, but they look away
when they are faced with cadmium and lead.

This farm was hailed the wonder of the age
the first to which ecology would bring
salvation: maybe that is why the sedge
is withered by the pond and no birds sing.

No wonder London folk who try to settle
here in the country bring the town with them
buying their water in a plastic bottle
and asking where their cabbages come from.

Their rude forefathers tilled the land, then turned
their aching backs on furrow, horse and plough
while these have come full circle and returned
to sleep in hamlets, watch their gardens grow.

East of them meanwhile through old Middlesex
the Grand Union lays its liquid rod
due north to Uxbridge, narrowing at locks
whose worn bricks mark where longboat people trod

ridged quadrants opening and closing gates
and at hump bridges still with tow-rope grooves
and widening to pass decayed estates
deserted factories, forgotten wharves.

BIRMINGHAM – BRENTFORD – SLOUGH: the rusty sign
beside an iron bridge bearded with grass
points north, south, west into the setting sun
from Cowley Peachey where no man may pass.

Dead tree-trunks, rotting hulks: it is all over
for the Slough Arm, whose stagnant waters lie
where horses hauled their barges out of cover
to ride an aqueduct against the sky.

This is the Green Belt, named for its decay:
the stream below the aqueduct will fall
here into Thorney Mill where small boys play
beside a parapet, a crumbling wall

with high blind windows. Find a gap, climb through
towards the sound of rushing water: step
carefully, for the water does not know
the mill is now a ruin. See it creep

towards the stone threshold, then slide across
and plunge into the millrace, round and down
under the iron wheel that lets it pass
rusted rigid, its wooden paddles gone.

'Where's Pocock's Lane?' Planes overhead, a queue
of hooting cars bound for the motorway:
so many people passing through, so few
to think of Pocock, John. 'Straight on', I say.

15

Words Against the Night

for Harry Guest

'Nasty old night' a dark shape said
as we passed each other on the lonely road
that wet November evening.

From under my umbrella
I mumbled something back, surprised
that here where lorries roar by day
bringing the city nearer, drowning speech
stranger should speak to stranger
that the vowels should be like turnips with the soil
still on them, that the speaker
should risk that friendly 'old': these were indeed
words against the night, a charm
to keep the ancient cold, the dark at bay
but a ritual too, a versicle
dropped into the silence
demanding a response.

16

Petition

> for *Valerie Bosley*

Lady, the leaves are catching fire in the avenue
the wattle fence around the estate is in need of repair
the stags have done their belling, the hinds are three months
    in calf
and I am not so young as I was. Man and boy
I have lived in this country cloister, this fair park
with its great house of Tudor chimneys and colonnades
where I have wiped my boots and made my prompt report
of deer, of poachers apprehended, of suckers lopped
of branches angled from the pond before the east
windows, and beside the house the darling church
topped with a spire you can see for miles that seems to tug it
heavenward, its nave no longer than its transepts, windows
whose tracery of leaf shapes these six hundred years
has writhed and wrestled in the pentecostal gale
its fine stone floor I sweep, keeping the commandments
always, and twice on Sunday and twice more during the
    week
lighting forty-seven candles, laying out vestments, finding
the place in the book, pulling the bell, pumping the organ:
WHEREAS your sweet self has visited me, stepping over
my threshold at the gate, brought into my room such light
as I had never dreamed the multitude of cobwebs
nor guessed the wealth of dust my dutiful years have
    gathered
whereas the fragrance of your tall and cheerful progress
has gusted through the trees I hold in trust, whose many
colours I had mistaken for my early autumn
until they flared before your laughter but did not fall
whereas you have expressed concern at the state of the fence
not for my lord's sake but for mine, whereas you know
a tine from a royal like no other woman I have met

whereas the man I am is belling as never before
WHEREFORE be pleased to accept my honourable services
vegetables, fruit and nuts from my small garden, hares
shot as they nibbled my lord's fence, whose ancestor
would poach the German king by running him hard at the
    hunt
wherefore know that I who am neither lord nor poacher
hunt the deer You, my lips pursed to summon the gentle
hounds of my earnest wishes, their panting calendar
cooled but in no wise chilled by your own more temperate
    seasons.
GIVEN at my hand this day, your birthday. My compliments
to your brother who knows his letters better than I.

17

Upton Park

The old Welsh metre rings true
rhyming yet seeming not to
like leaves on the burning tree
jagged when taken singly
but from only two we learn
the beginnings of pattern
a pattern we also share
as fellow heirs of nature
in this garden like the one
God first planted in Eden
where he put the man to name
his world like himself, Adam
for each kind, Marvell said once
does streight its own resemblance
find in a garden.   The tongue
leaflike is always turning
fiery, not to die or kill
for its laws are more subtle
but to set glowing apart
by a creative effort
to divide lawns with a hedge
and to tame the more savage
growth that it may bear more fruit
to prune but not inhibit
like a hand trimming a wick
that the flame may more frolic
for the tongue, this flaming sword
cuts the silence that severed
you from me, each other's kind
although we never listened!

18

On a Theme of James Joyce

Tell me
tell me
tell me
   elm

whom storm
never
over-
   whelmed

why has
autumn
come so
   soon?

   This
autumn
will bring
no spring.

   Worm
drilled me
filled me
killed me.

   Man
fell me
fell me
fell me.

19

The Chimney

Brick by brick
it rose into the sky
and John, Frank, Alf, George and Vic

watched: nine months they watched
the growing of the chimney
for the boilers for the greenhouses
for these are five green-fingered men

who all their lives have dibbled
pricked out, tamped, pegged down
staked, pruned, grafted, watered
waited.
      Fifty years later
the greenhouses have gone
five men have grown old
and now the land is to be sold:
in six seconds their chimney

topples from the sky
and John, Frank, Alf, George and Vic
watch it die.

20

Saga

The father
I walked from Sticklepath to find a wife.
I was fed up with all the dairy work
and met this girl: her father had a greenhouse
and I offered to give his buds a wash.
She didn't mind, and I was not embarrassed.
She fell for me and soon we had a son.

The mother
Even as a girl I had wanted a son
but in our village you were first a wife
and then a mother. I was that embarrassed.
But father found dad – that's my husband – work.
It's funny how things come out in the wash.
We left the aphids to it in the greenhouse.

The son
Sometimes it feels like living in a greenhouse
with 'One day all this will be yours, my son.'
All what? A little house, a car to wash.
Now all I have to do is find a wife.
Well, there's a girl friend: I meet her from work
and bring her home. She's awkward here, embarrassed.

The daughter
Number two, me: I need not be embarrassed
for I was not begotten in a greenhouse.
I passed exams: now I do office work
and spend my evenings with a grocer's son.
Next week he will ask me to be his wife
and that will mean to serve, to cook, to wash.

The grandmother
The boy's my favourite: but will she wash
his socks and cook, and never be embarrassed?
This smart new girl he's got – is she a wife

to share his life, his interests, his greenhouse
if he gets one? Will she give him a son
to carry on whatever is his work?

The girl friend
I don't think for a moment it would work.
Although he tries hard, bless him, it won't wash
with daddy. Lose a daughter, gain a son . . .
but I'm quite certain they would be embarrassed.
I dream of a red garden, a green house,
croquet and friends – and me the loving wife?

The neighbours
He needs a wife who will go out to work –
not in a greenhouse. Debts? They'll be awash.
Embarrassed? Better dry out in the sun.

21

Waters Above

Here were pastures, cornfields, farms, familiar landscape:
now this hill has swelled like a smooth improbable tumour
dwarfing several villages, beauty spots cheated of beauty
all for the sake of the distant capital's water requirements.
Still, because it is there we will climb and see what it looks
    like.

Passing sheep on the slope that briefly pause in their grazing
blankly look and bleating return to what they are there for
father and small son tramp up towards a level horizon
where of a sudden we find ourselves in seaside surroundings:
this then is where those gulls live which have invaded our
    garden
even in summer, scaring away our thrushes and blackbirds!
Strangers to lakes, we stare at acres of glittering water
with, at the furthest edge, those spires and chimneys we
    know of:
all our world is reversed, transfigured by waters above it.

Yes, it is good to be here, but we must go back to the valley
which, we are soon to discover, has otherwise not been
    exalted:
and we descend with rippling hearts like favoured apostles
or like Moses, his face translucent as horn, to the village
where we began, where we live, where no one wants to
    believe us.

22

Knowing the desert places of the heart —
Rusted machines on land nobody tills —
You found the quarry exhausted too, the mill's
Sluices jammed solid, and made a fresh start.

The problem round this way is likewise dead
Years, empty spaces, silted streams, no labour:
No less having an airport for a neighbour
And national prestige low overhead.

*Well, heart or not, you left it all behind.
How can I tell you what is on my mind?
You can see I am not beyond repair . . .*

Now as I try, my heart grows desolate:
Oh, what's the use when promises so grate
That you shake decibels out of your hair?

23

Slough Station: Broad Gauge

Seven feet and a quarter of an inch
from rail to rail, the wooden sleepers laid
end to end under them: down such a road
Brunel's tall engines strutted on great wheels
with copper bands aflame on their funnels
coaches agleam in chocolate and cream.
That was Great Western, that was style.
                                                Meanwhile
the others took the width of a coal truck
in some benighted northern mine, made it
the standard gauge, laid sleepers side by side:
Brunel was bolder, faster, smoother, better
(the coin stood on edge in the dining-car
has never fallen over) but he was
alone.
        If we are to be guests of each
other, there comes a time when we
must shrink from broad to standard gauge
and we shall tell ourselves the world
missed the chance we gave it to be
perfect: but the permanent way
of course remains, the bed of stones
on which our style is balanced still.

24

At Datchet Station

Four foot eight and three-eighths, the track is true
the trackman says, or as we have to say
in millimetres now, one-four-three-two.

His orange waistcoat never lost from view
steady his step and permanent his way:
four foot eight and three-eighths, the track is true.

With his notched stick he puts the metals through
his paces, stooping now and then to lay
in millimetres now, one-four-three-two

from rail to rail. Look, I protest, I grew
up on the railway. Your stick leads astray –
four foot eight and three-eighths. The track is true

at four foot eight and a half, or I'm askew.
I don't care what it was, sir, in your day:
in millimetres now, one-four-three-two.

And he plods off as one who always knew
that those gone off the rails have hell to pay.
Four foot eight and three-eighths, the track is true:
in millimetres now, one-four-three-two.

25

Departure

The rest is silence, Hamlet says
and is no more. Perhaps it is
like pulling out of Datchet on
an empty train and sitting down
while the platform diminishes

to dishes, to a wife who lays
things in a sink after goodbyes
glad that with husband, children gone
      the rest is silence –

a milkman plodding his strait ways
a baker loading bread on trays
a teacher bidding small feet run
and an old man mowing a lawn:
perhaps beyond the fields and skies
      the rest is silence.

26

Ulysses

For thirty years, a generation
he left behind, he travelled
no trackless way but up
and down the London and North-Eastern.
Twice a week, in uniform
he inspected trains and never got off
for a keepsake of Peterborough
nor for a strange dish at Grantham, he avoided
the stare of a one-eyed man at Newark
and the knives of Retford: Doncaster
did not make a beast of him but sent him on
to York where he met old friends, the girls
of Darlington neither chewed nor swallowed him
while after Berwick-on-Tweed he went alone
to Edinburgh where he turned round
and came back.   At Ithaca now
he spends his days in the public library
making himself an expert on local history
and his nights in the old folk's home.

27

Doris

Between a warehouse long overgrown with weeds
and buildings long since used as a factory
    she waits and sighs while her admirers
  photograph her and discuss their passion

with one another: this is the day she makes
her final journey down to her rendezvous
    and after all this time she surely
  knows every inch of the way and loves it.

Reporters armed with pencils and writing-pads
are talking to her driver, who climbs aboard
    consults her instruments, declares her
  ready to go and her sighing ceases:

he backs her, couples her to a line of trucks
and Doris, none the worse for her fifty years
    is on the job once more, enjoying
  (if it is possible) every moment.

She whistles and moves off to a clang of bells,
a flash of lights, a shouting of little boys:
    look, here she comes with clouds ascending!
  Warehouse and factory walls are booming

then out she thunders into the open, past
the bays, the cooling-towers and over an
    ungated level crossing with its
  pin-up of her on a rusty railing:

she sings to grind round corners, she takes the points
with ease, her six-wheeled stride is as good as new
    but she is holding up the traffic
  whatever else may be going for her.

She carries empties not to be filled again.
Tomorrow men will rip up her track and lay
    a road, a pipeline: Doris will be
  taken away to be scrapped or pampered.

Before her smoke can get in our eyes, the wind
is filled with sweetness: into a factory
    where chocolate is made a lorry
  pumps a consignment of liquid sugar.

28

Alpha Street

When a body overtakes
the sound it makes
                BOOM
so to this boom town
under a flight path
they come from where milk
had four legs and bread a crust
but there was not enough
of either, to start afresh
in Alpha Street: Alpha Street
is always with us, though
last year it was condemned.

Reprieved this year, flush
with grants to update
Victorian hygiene
houses celebrate
with bijou bow windows
looking straight on to the street
porticoes adorned
with coaching-lamps leading
straight into living-rooms
and with a new coat of paint:
even the brickwork is
pink and mauve, picked out in white.

Tonight on his low front wall
that boasted railings
before the war, a man
in cloth cap, carpet
slippers sits with legs
crossed in threadbare trousers
no collar, no tie, no teeth
his weathered hand cupping
a limp cigarette.

He gets on all right with them
but he wouldn't have wanted
his daughter to marry
one of the laughing men
a few doors down, standing
on the pavement outside
the Public Bar, for there is
no other, their pork pie hats
tilted back
          their wives
in overalls, thick arms
folded with one hand stroking
the chin, call to each other
like tropical birds, their sons
up late, preparing
for man's estate, play
cricket against a wall
under a streetlamp
their elder daughters run
hooting, filling the twilight
with white lace and awkward
bodies
        and high above
a man clambers on beams
climbs among rafters:
his old slate roof is off
and he renews his woodwork
by the light of a bulb
that glows nakedly –
a heart behind bared ribs.

Doubtless one day they will
move away and Alpha Street
will be condemned once more
part of the dying heart
of a town already old
spreading outward in layers
like an old yew tree.

29

The Brush

In the no man's land
between the village
and the factories
a new pub
        THE BRUSH
atop a tall pole
its sign, the likeness
of a fox in scrap
metal
    spare parts for
a head, bodywork
and crankshafts turned back
to what they were called
after
    and a tail
from a dynamo
brush: it was too much
for the locals who
took potshots at it

so the brewery
had it taken down
and renamed the pub
THE COACH AND HORSES.

31

The Writing on the Wall

MAN UNTED says the writing on the wall.
Is this a coded message that a NUN
has just been MATED? We are on the ball
believing that MEN DAUNT, but just for fun
on this occasion when the score is one
all and the theme no more than ANENT MUD.
So, MAN, stay TUNED: no collar and no stud
adorns the writer's shirt, and little schooling
his close-cropped skull. But hobnailed boots tread blood
where there's no wall to write on. I'm not fooling.

31

Arson

That night the sky was red
with the wooden schoolhouse
and in the morning
                       a map
of pipes and radiators
marked where classroom walls
had been
             a parallelogram
of charred beams was scratched
across the sky
                 water went on
finding its own level
dripping
         from a storage tank
while at the entrance the mock
stone pillars were barely
touched
           and across the playing-field
papers
      papers
             were blown about
or held against the chainlink fence
the boundary of citizens'
gardens
       A DAY IN THE LIVE
OF A BUS DRIVER
                 I would like
to be a docter
         'unrealistic
aims'
     scattered
             to the wind
hanging around street corners
where fire no longer purifies
but makes hell-mouths and hydra-heads.

32

The Potter's Field

We with shovels and sacks move among little hills:
this was where long ago rubbish was laid to rest
    just below the embankment
where today the canal is still.

Barges creaked on their ropes bringing from London smoke
twenty miles to the east out to this country place
    droppings, rich droppings from the
first consumer society.

Man has moulded this land, shaped it and dunged it too
once already and left tree-trunks and flourishing
    thistles, and he returns this
Sunday morning to mould it once

more, a century past: see how the little hills
raised by dustmen of old hop to their children's strains
    here and there as the shovels
bring rejoicing on every side!

What was rubbish to them may be antiques for us.
Start to dig anywhere: anywhere it will clink.
    Twist the shovel and out will
tumble bottles and jugs and jars.

You can tell by the shape – this was for Bovril once –
or the name has survived, baked underneath the glaze.
    Look: Frank Cooper of Oxford –
that can only be marmalade.

On my desk as I write, holding some paper clips
Plumtree's Home Potted Meats, sold in a can today
    not this elegant object –
that is, if they are sold at all.

We who strip to the waist, what do we really want?
Here we are in this field, call it the Potter's Field:
    it is full of ceramics
  and for burying strangers in.

But it cannot produce anything but remains:
dust was never so red as our inheritance.
    When we hit upon something
  it is pearls that were someone's eyes.

33

Corpus Christi

In the less fashionable part of town
among the factories and workers' houses
a small park hums with hoop-la, beer, ice-cream:
at the far edge, above the fence, a flag
flaps on a mast for there is the canal
forgotten by all save anglers and small boys
between deserted wharves and overgrown
banks till today.
              Today a carnival
declares whole decades scythed and dredged away
and the canal, bobbing with rivercraft
open for pleasure.
              In the park a voice
summons us to an old furniture van
with one side out – a stage: three men and a girl
in speech and song, flat cap and apron tell
the tale of the canals, the toil, the sweat
of carving trade routes through a sleepy land
reminding us of lives made and unmade
in longboats bright with painted spiky flowers
and grimy children.
              In the Middle Ages
it was the Fall, the Rising: today no less
it is the clearing of a way by water
from heart to heart, a quickening of the air.

34

You mention my canal. A Londoner
suddenly you are in my neighbourhood:
you lived here in a longboat once and brewed
soup from the nettle, wine from the elderflower.

Here you were part of someone's dream – you still
bear his name – but your own dream soon was wrecked.
The water failed to move: did you expect
a river? It is only a canal.

Back now in London and alone, you have
pot-plants all round you, one red rose I gave.
Could we not open up a thoroughfare

between your house and mine, along the Thames
whose motion would keep fresh all future dreams?
But you are shaking petals from your hair.

35

Mr Holmes

Yes, I remember Mr Holmes:
his house stood, rickety and tall
at the corner of Bellevue Place
where the vue was not belle at all.

On the ground floor he kept his shop
and lived behind it: bedrooms, attic
were now beyond a man who thought
the damp was making him asthmatic.

A long low shed filled his back yard:
here was his kneading-trough, the old
back-breaking oven where he baked
the crisp and crusty loaves he sold.

His shop was always full, he knew
in what regard the village held him
but though we flourished on his wares
the flour got on his chest and killed him.

And yet we almost envy him
for as the office blocks rise higher
like steam-baked bread, our lives grow stale:
he was the last to live by fire.

36

Seed Merchant

Signor mio car, I step
into your shop to buy
a sack of meal
for my four spinster hens
and a fragrance
hits me at the door: grain
whole and milled, dried herbs,
fertiliser – all summer
remembered, promised.
                       With you
at the far end, flanked
by dog biscuits and bird seed
the window behind your head
framing you as you stand
behind the counter, this could be
the temple of some scandalous
cult, and you
with your ruddy face and sun-bleached hair
its John Barleycorn.

37

Market

FISH IS WILD AND PURE!
STRAIGHT FROM THE COLD SEA!
OUR FISHERMEN ARE HUNTERS
THEY WORK WITH COURAGE TO CAPTURE
THE LEANEST CLEANEST FOOD
                              scrawled
on a blackboard propped against a row of slabs
of cod, squid, coley, red mullet, whelks, winkles
but next door (though there are no doors here)
red letters shaded black proclaim
DELHI EMPORIUM
                   and you walk among
mangoes, yams, lady's fingers, curry pastes
for those in a hurry, while those at home
send out their husbands to sneeze among
ground coriander, turmeric, dried
fenugreek, sold here as homelier
dhania, haldi, methi
                   Out again
and into where a lady calls you mister
her accent grated Parmesan, her eyes
disappointed olives
                   A greengrocer
picks up a pair of melons, makes a face
as a pretty girl goes by: PLEASE DON'T SQUEEZE ME
UNTIL I'M YOURS, a display
of tomatoes murmurs
                   Puppies yelp
goldfish gulp, canaries preen, guppies
inquire, mynahs can't cope, budgerigars
couldn't care less, kittens stagger
drugged with the world, guinea-pigs have always
just got up
            but here a young butcher
chops off a pheasant's (yes, a pheasant's)
wing feathers, puts down his chopper

and fans the feathers out across his hand
(pale brown flecked with cream, rooted
in a speck of red) smiling:
a present for his child
                        and opposite
an elderly couple with glottal speech
and impeccable courtesy
sell handbags, wallets, purses, no sir, we
do not sell lampshades
                        Pause, however
briefly, before tits, chewing-gum, bums
badges (I AM A VIRGIN) dolly mixtures
rubber goods, YOUR DOG'S NAME ENGRAVED
FREE, I wonder what's behind there:
Can I help you, sir
                KEEP ME GOING, LORD
a plaque implores on behalf of a rival
watching over his table mats whose Arcs
de Triomphe, Eiffel Towers demand
a *couvert* of cutlery from China
china from nowhere in particular
(cover it, cover it) Pure Crystal
glasses, teapots, toothpicks
doubling as cocktail sticks, a chrome
menorah, a pair of hand-drums:
the pious owner nods his dreadlocks
to throbbing reggae
                        A passing schoolboy
taps out a beat on the drums, remembering
a land he has never seen
                        A man
in dark glasses and surely deaf as well
dribbles 'Love's last word is spoken'
through a battered saxophone, playing
for pennies among pounds of freezer meat.

38

Pastoral

Come live with me and be my love
for I am desperate to prove
that coming all this lonely way for
a job has something in its favour.

Tonight the wind is north-west, bearing
sweetness: a group of us are sharing
a room and each night all of us
go off to Mars the marvellous

to pack up chocolates to send
money to all of you. We spend
our days in cafés where they cook
as mother did, and then we look

at Lata while she sings her way
through to some hero's smile: we say
life is not like that, but at least
in famine we can see a feast.

Or else we go for walks to while
the hours away, in single file
because the paths are narrow round
the flowerbeds of the Pleasure Ground

then home to where our beds are stacked
in rows. One man would have us backed
by a trade union, but I don't
fully follow his argument.

Some lucky fellows have their wives
already here: one of them thrives.
I hope this money is enough.
Please live with me and be my love.

39

To Take Away

Under a calendar that shows a girl
with downcast eyes wearing everything
but a veil and an envelope stuck on the wall
bearing the handwritten trilingual legend
NO POLITICS PLEASE THANK YOU a boy
in a white coat too big for him presides
over pyramids of home-made confections
orange yellow off-white and on good days green
a tray of chopped onions with a bowl of brown
sauce beside another tray of vegetables
battered to spicy anonymity
and a third tray of small triangular pies
an array of steaming canisters where curries
mature a few scrawny chickens whose bare flesh
glows a dull parched delicious red a bed
of switched-on charcoal on which the boy
turns and roasts meat cakes he calls kababs
and when they are done pops into a foil-lined bag
whose mouth puffs steam as he closes it and smiling
hands the feast to me.

40

Mr Gunn

SUPPORT YOUR LOCAL POET said
the fairground badge, and just for fun
I bought it, thought it merited
an airing, so I pinned it on
my coat: let friends and colleagues shun
frivolity and turn away.
I prefer currants in my bun:
not every poet rhymes this way.

I donned my coat and decked my head
for there was little sign of sun
and took my shoes for a retread
to where repairs are neatly done
soles healed beyond comparison.
You must believe me when I say
the cobbler is a Mr Gunn:
not every poet rhymes this way.

He looked up from his wax and thread:
'A poet, eh? I had begun
to wonder how you earn your bread.'
He filled his mouth with nails, and one
by one his rasp slammed a bright run
of dots around a shoe. 'Wednesday?
My favourite is Tennyson:
not every poet rhymes this way.'

ENVOY

Good Mr Gunn, these lines I've spun
Uphold their feet as best they may.
Now you, I know, please everyone:
Not every poet rhymes this way.

41

Tradesmen

Without the butcher
what would the baker do for meat

without the baker
how would the candlestick-maker
mop up his gravy

without the candlestick-maker
how would the butcher and the baker
and their hard-pressed wives
and their many children
light their way to bed

but without the poet
life would go on much as ever
at least for his fellow tradesmen

as soon as the poet realises this
his poems will improve.

42

Last Spring

The slow spring evenings
saw her at her gate
her daughter in bed
her man working late:

while birds sang she talked
with neighbours and friends
laughing with her eyes
waving her white hands

her long hair shining
loose in the warm breeze
her good breasts moving
in a linen blouse.

September sees her
out with her household –
proud husband, daughter
and a newborn child

her nylon suit, gloves
neat hair and pluckt brow
signals to the world:
'We've shut up shop now.'

43

Cat and Sick Child

We understand with speech
        our hedge
dividing path and lawn

but he stands under words
        sheltered
by them and innocent

able to go where we
        cannot –
through gaps in hedges, up

poles and tree-trunks, between
        reasons:
pure furry unreason

going straight to the heart
        of the
matter, teeth and claws in

the bird's flesh, asking no
        questions
or tongue and paws on this

girl's skin, knowing she is
        injured
licking her slow fingers

tickling them back to sense
        treading
her body to laughter

healing her, creature to
        creature
without speaking of love.

44

An Irishwoman Visits Her Son

The Old Woman of Beare
felt the tide ebb away
but I with my white hair
am up early today

sweeping my son's front path
in a fine neighbourhood.
Thank you, we are well both:
life was never so good

since with his father I
drove the cows out to pasture
and myself was not dry
before my young sweet master.

Let that Old Woman be
chewing the cud of prayer:
I need no rosary
now I am living here

my fingers round no beads
but my hands round a broom
all my thoughts, words and deeds
making his kingdom come.

Let that Old Woman moan
that kings once kissed her hand:
I do not moan alone
along a lengthening strand

for I took to the waves
and almost am reborn
sweeping away the leaves
and mending what is torn.

My daughter-in-law walked out
taking the children with her:
a man can do without
while he still has a mother

to keep him ironed and aired
and neat and good as new.
Our Blessed Lady cared:
my son has talents too.

Seven o'clock. I hear
a bedroom window slam:
but they would give a cheer
to know how glad I am!

45

Man of Letters

P. ALLEN said
black letters shaded red
above his head: HAIRDRESSER
TOBACCONIST, he filled his low
doorway in old Chalvey.

To his left three gothick panes
offered in the same untaught hand
HAIRCUTTING SHAMPOOING SHAVING
with SINGEING added further down
the middle pane:
                        to his right
a faded cardboard face
with glossy hair said PLAYERS PLEASE
and a notice gave the times
of buses and steamers
that had stopped running years before.

I lived opposite: both of us
men of letters, Percy and I
watched each other across
what was still called the High Street
and waited for the angel.

Sometimes I was his angel
stepping low into the fragrant
gloom of the last shop, asking for
his short back and sides, refusing
what he called Saturday nights.

Now that his shop and lonely house
from which he drove twelve yards to work
are gone and he is past caring
he is my angel and I set
these letters on his poem's glass.

46

Listen, this town where you were once a shopper
is full of people yearning to belong
and longing to be free: this way they throng
from tyrannies, and that is right and proper.

Your parents felt the same and put roots down
not far from here: they brought you up to speak
two languages, and nowadays you seek
where you belong – surely not in this town.

Listen, I want you to belong to me:
I am no tyrant, you would still be free
and we would go together anywhere.

But neither refugee nor immigrant
you will not recognise my tyrant want
shaking my heavy hand out of your hair.

47

In Memory of Sid Osborne

Shehecheyanu:
you found the word in a folk song
about a new baby? Well, it means
'who hast kept us in life'
and it comes from the blessing
for the firstfruits of the season –
not for what is new
                (he loves
talking to customers, and sprung
from a nation of scholar
tailors, taxi drivers, money
lenders, carpenters even, can make
a point of law, especially
after a question, last from clippers
to brush)
        but for what is
renewed: a baby is no
novelty! Or take the mother
after what you would call her churching
though by us she takes a real bath
when she is lying there all sweet and fresh . . .
why, then her husband will say
shehecheyanu.

48

General Practitioner

From lands where they
stamped out Old Prussian
and centuries later carted
Yiddish off in trains

where Germans have Polish names
and Poles have German names
                                      Tadeusz
Niedenthal came to sit at a small desk
in a back room overlooking the dead
garden of a suburban house converted
into a surgery
                taking temperatures
and using the silence
to read his mail through steel-rimmed spectacles

looking up with an embarrassed smile
to wave one of 'zees holiday post cards'
his careful hand prescribing aspirin
for yet another strapping square-faced patient

reaching up for a solemn handshake
and down for his flask of bitter coffee.

49

Lulu

Blown about the autumn streets
yellow red purple
not leaves but Lulu
in her sad rags
tottering in plimsolls

her once bleached hair
ill held in a flimsy scarf
her eyes made up for nightmare
cheeks and lips of a doll
clutching a carrier bag

meeting the trains every night
scanning the faces
which looked away
touting for customers
we used to say

but when she died
one winter dawn
in the garden of a man
who wanted to marry her
he told the papers

of an Estonian
refugee who had lost
her husband and son
in the war and never stopped
hoping to find them again.

50

The Bogomils

The Bogomils
with their wrestling gods
Good and Evil
were simple folk

they did not sing or dance
or paint or write
or make things to last

only cups plates that broke
spoons knives that wore out
clothes that turned to rags
huts that fell down

nor did they even
reproduce themselves
that was all of the world

so devout they died out
all that is left of them
is gravestones depicting
men with raised right hands

the Bogomils
with their distinctive cry
smrt smrt

are still with us
simple folk welders
milkmen labourers
living in hostels

waiting for the call
clutching old passports
in their raised right hands.

51

The Wedding Guest

<blockquote>for Miķēlis Mežmalietis</blockquote>

Among the wedding guests
a short stout man with a white beard
and a twinkle in his eye:
there is nothing he has not seen or heard

before, and now he stands with these
youngsters framed by relatives
and a gothick arch with flowers
attendant, and hopes their lives

will be better served by history
and one fine but later day
he will tell them of a future
history tossed away

not out of self pity
but as a warning
of what they could wake up to find
one morning.

In January '43 (he will say)
    because I had not enlisted
in the German occupying forces
    I was arrested

and thrown into Valmiera camp
    with common criminals
starving Russians, German deserters
    still wearing their medals.

Twenty months later we were sent
    to Riga, where a boat
took us across the Amber Sea
    to Danzig and our fate.

On a freight train they loaded us
    fifty men to a truck:
when a man died the SS guards
    dropped him beside the track.

Sincerity, Sacrifice and Love
    met us at Sachsenhausen:
the Iron Crosses were ripped off
    and their owners stood frozen

naked each morning in the yard
    in the late October wind
while fire hoses purged them of lice
    and glory left behind.

One-three-seven-five-four-six
    was me for ten days, then
they marched us to a Heinkel factory
    and thousands of other men.

Numbers, not names we were, except
    for groups of Polish nobles
who still had their servants with them:
    these, despite their troubles

would have wash basins brought to them
    with water ready poured
and they would wipe their delicate hands
    on linen fit for a lord.

We were locked in the hangars to sleep
    on sawdust and concrete
and the frost bit uncovered toes
    on rows of wood-shod feet.

'Blow, wind . . .': we sang the ancient song
    huddled on a little hill.
The other nations who had no songs
    gathered and stood still.

'Blow, wind . . .': but only half of us
    were left after one night
when a bomber aimed at a hangar
    and scored a direct hit.

'Blow, wind . . .': the flower of Latvia –
    young intellectuals
who when the Russians had marched in
    had lost their teeth and nails.

From there to Meppen, where we slept
    in a barn with a leaking roof:
outside, two prisoners swung for a week
    to warn runaways off.

We dug trenches, machine-gun nests
    never intended for use
and while we worked, low-flying planes
    would take pot shots at us.

Dysentery struck: the SS guards
    would make the sickest men
wash their trousers in a ditch
    and put them on again

still wet, so that in minutes they
    and the men inside them froze.
Every evening we brought them back
    piled up on wheelbarrows

rigid as rhubarb, their bare feet
    sticking out either side
for boots were the only legacy
    a man left when he died.

Spring saw us at Neuengamme
    and covered up her face:
we were the last and dying slaves
    of a doomed master race.

*He will offer home-made sausage
pickled gherkins and brandy
with news of a song festival:
he has the programme handy*

*among scattered records, books
by Rainis, Skalbe, in a room
full of happier days remembered –
a scrap of national costume*

*hanging from a nail, a young soldier
in a forgotten uniform, a picnic,
a church tower among trees, the president
of a forgotten republic*

*a string instrument of white wood,
The Daily Telegraph open
at the foreign news page . . . fragments
of a twenty-one-year honeymoon.*

At the end of April '45
    (he will go on) it was settled
that we would board ships at Lübeck, sail
    and in an hour be scuttled –

or so I heard, but many plans
    were to go awry that week:
they loaded us on a passenger liner
    commandeered from a rich Greek.

Carpets and mirrors and chandeliers!
    We wondered where we were . . .
but in seconds I was asleep
    in a deep upholstered chair.

With fourteen thousand men on board
    the ship was overset
so some of us must change our class
    from passenger to freight.

The stronger made the weaker cross
    to the dark bulk alongside:
between *Cap Arcona* and *Athenas*
    a plank stretched, inches wide.

On deck neat stacks of something stood
    under tarpaulin sheets:
below, two empty holds for us
    with floors of metal plates.

And while our ship churned through the night
    in our own filth we lay
starving, then with no drinking water
    by the second day.

Typhoid had first choice: to our hold –
    the lower, near the keel –
they brought the bodies from above
    and added them to our pile.

I crawled across to them, and they
    became my mattress, for
at least they were warmer, drier, softer
    than that metal floor.

But their lice were still alive, and they
    enjoyed a change of host:
you could scoop them up in handfuls where
    they clustered about your waist.

The intellectuals died first
    but all of us had become
like our own vermin, crawling, clawing
    tumbling in that foul gloom.

The ship had moved in fits and starts
    and then on the fourth day
explosions thudded all around
    both near and far away

till one enough to split your skull
    sent a strong man up to look:
the Yanks had sunk our sister ship
    he said when he came back.

Nobody told us – how could they? –
    that the war would soon be won:
they thought our ships were full of Nazis
    seeking a place in the sun.

Perhaps they would bomb us next, and our
    sufferings would be at an end:
but the ship lurched, then shuddered to a stop
    for we had put in to land.

We were at Neustadt: those who could
    climbed out and stepped ashore
and I alone was left for dead
    with my mattress-mates on the floor.

Sometimes we are afraid of you
as if you knew too much
from going to the pit and back
so that when you touch

less travelled lives like ours
you burn
and we are scarred with a knowledge
from which there is no return:

but our mass-production century
has also mass produced
Tiresias and the Wandering Jew
who for all our sakes must

tell, for henceforth silence is
not golden but leaden
and therefore poisonous
and nothing more must be hidden.

I could not move (he will soon be done)
    but lay among the dead
and for about an hour and a half
    I heard no voice nor tread.

I dragged myself up on deck. Those stacks
    had been slashed open and spilled:
sugar, rice, macaroni, flour –
    while we starved in the hold!

But I was thirsty. I found a barrel
    of pickled beetroot near:
I leaned over and drank, and drank
    whole quarts of vinegar.

When I came round, I heard a language
    I did not understand:
two French students were looking for spoils
    but it was me they found.

They carried me to a deserted barracks
    where they occupied a room:
they deloused me, washed me, put me to bed
    but I could not swallow a crumb.

Round my bed was their loot – watches,
    cameras, jewellery:
when visitors called while they were out
    my screams scared them away.

Two weeks I stayed there, while outside
    the Allies won the war:
my friends went home, the hospital
    at last had room for more.

He's small, but he has broad shoulders
    and he can work, they said:
after two years in hospital
    we were stood on parade

before some tweedy Englishwomen
    sent to recruit cheap labour
and that is why you have a bloody
    foreigner for a neighbour.

A foreigner I shall always be
    alone with many friends
but these and music and my garden
    can never make amends

for a small nation sick to death
    the heart knocked out of me:
the German plague is over now
    the Russian will never be

and I who was your wedding guest
    am here to give a warning
lest you should lose all that I lost
    as a young man one morning.

52

We have discussed the Seven Trances, tried
one or two, sat with hands linked round a table
consulted zodiacs, palms, a formidable
tome which explained just who was crucified.

You are a gift from God, an envious friend
enlightens me: too seldom is it given
thus to transcend the body, float to heaven
with a choice spirit, hand in cool white hand.

I am your heretic — neither Gnostic nor
Nestorian, but a worshipper of your
person, and gasping in this upper air

I long to go out shopping with you, ask
the price of apples: you take me to task
and shake my grosser unction from your hair.

53

Sister

Every day from school she collects her children:
classic English beauty she is, with golden
hair, blue eyes, face peaches and cream, though maybe
    somewhat old-fashioned

with her headscarf even in blazing summer
and her gaze cast down when a man approaches,
high-necked blouse, no frills, and a skirt that almost
    reaches her ankles.

Once she brings her husband along – that man who
in the High Street Saturday afternoons stands
eyes agleam and lips with a line of spittle
    thumping a Bible.

54

Shared Church

Ein' feste Burg our square grey church
    with narrow slits for windows:
the local vandals vainly search
    for damageable splendours.
        The neighbourhood is tough
        but this is tough enough
        to keep toughs in their place
        or turn them to embrace
the faith and its defenders.

This was the first church of its kind:
    they told us we were foolish
to think the Irish would not mind
    while Mass was said in Polish.
        And then the Anglicans
        sing hymns and read the banns
        for we have equal shares
        in property and prayers
that no power shall demolish.

The ground plan is a fat Greek cross
    and space is quite elastic:
when folk can slide the walls across
    they grow enthusiastic.
        For anything that comes
        we can make room, make rooms:
        to meet the Lord's demands
        see, at our centre stands
a font in local plastic.

55

Period Wedding

London and South-Western coaches
    gliding out of Waterloo!
Clapham past, the Thames approaches:
    here is Richmond, there is Kew.
Twickenham, Whitton: you have written
    'Please be here by half past two'.

Green the train and green the country-
    side it rocks and rattles through:
discontent with only one tree
    in a backyard with no view
you have picked a fast Invicta
    and a cottage – just like you!

Feltham, Ashford, Staines and into
    sleepy Buckinghamshire: few
are the places I have been to
    where the sky is quite so blue
and the river makes you give a
    sigh of pleasure. Yes, me too!

Your mamma has won – I know, dear:
    it was not a battle. True
love like ours (I love you so, dear)
    needs no far-off rendezvous:
let our dearest be our nearest
    and give credit where it's due.

Silver frames around the photos
    winking at you while you grew!
All those uncles in their motors
    honking down the avenue:

tails and toppers coming croppers
    saying things I wish I knew.

Now the wedding bells are ringing
    whispers fly from pew to pew:
your mamma amid the singing
    will slip in a soft boo-hoo
but you're mine now, so . . . I'm fine now
    and I'll stick to you like glue!

56

Gipsy Funeral

The church packed on a Thursday afternoon:
the other community is here. Menders
of roads, dealers in used cars and old clothes,
hawkers of nosegays gathered from the heath
by the canal: dark looks, thick hair, earrings
and three surnames between them.
                              The parson
raises his voice to heaven, his round vowels
to rafters: 'Let us say the Twenty-third
Psalm.' Nobody moves except the widow
who in the front pew gives herself to grief
as though to love. The parson's plain tenor
renders 'Abide with me' – all five verses.

Outside, the whole churchyard covered with wreaths
feet stumbling over gravestones, over one
another. Housewives, tradesmen, schoolchildren
stop, look and whisper. 'Ashes to ashes'
the parson says through cigarette smoke. A cross
of flowers thuds down. Harry has shed his wheels.

57

Hymn Tune Prelude
(VAUGHAN WILLIAMS)

Dear commonplaces! The light
touches the pews, the pulpit
and the warm air from the west
door at this time of harvest

thrills as the pipes speak, make way
in the maze of their many
voices for the single thread
of a hymn celebrated.

'Author of life divine' (words
to point the glad heart skywards)
'Who hast a table spread' (come
be lifted to the Kingdom)

'Furnished with mystic Wine' (flutes
fluttering on the high notes)
'And everlasting Bread' (tune
sung in broad diapason):

'Preserve the life thyself hast
given' (we shall not be lost)
'And feed and train us up for
heaven.' Still the tune is there –

Rhosymedre, lowly yarn
woven into the pattern
as the elements are blest
to bring in heaven's harvest.

Dear commonplaces that take
and underlay to music
our works and lives, light and air
filling the prayer we offer!

58

Two Minutes' Silence

for John and Frances Dodd

The missing leg or arm, they say, still itches:
but the pluckt eye is blind as ever now
as upright men pay tribute to their comrades
    somewhere under the plough.

That corner of a foreign field is not
for ever England to a bombardier:
he is a bit of France or Belgium now
    with poppies in his ear.

From the Old Lie to the eternal truth
we come this morning: 'They shall not grow old.'
Yes, they were Isaacs, but the ancient tale
    went wrong when it was told.

Today it is each man's right to grow old
to feel age weary him, the years condemn.
But some saw no alternative to dying:
    we must remember them.

We say they gave their lives: their lives were stolen
and we are still poor after sixty years
to speak of honour, leaving the flesh proud
    that might be healed with tears.

Knell, Minor, Doubles

59

LORD   LORD   LORD
says the great tenor
for a man, a year
passing
LORD   LORD   LORD
in thee have I trusted
let me never be
confounded
LORD   LORD   LORD
the thrice threefold stroke
of the Nine Tailors
the tellers, the tollers
the long thread of life
loosed from the clasping hand
to rise like reversed
lightning to the height
copper and tin blended
to thunder, to summon
to prayer, to remembrance
here at Langley Marish
of George full of years
of Edith after much
suffering, to ring
the old year out with twelve
strokes more, one for each month
then a peal to ring
the new year in, to call
to joy as long ago
at Upton when the folk
gathered at the smithy
to hear their heroine
Pamela married off
they pulled for her: today
we do likewise and trust
God to pull his weight, for
OUR HOPE IS IN THE LORD.

60

'Treble's going . . . it's gone':
two, then three, four and five
and deep tenor go down
into Plain, Treble Bob
or Grandsire or Stedman:
the ringers, like the bells
speak their own tongue that tells
of covers, courses, hunts
or stand silent half way
up the west tower, a ring
intent at six quick ropes'
ends of six young people –
men with shirtsleeves rolled back
to elbows (for is this
not harvest time in church?)
facing women who smile
and haul a cool blessing
with bare arms from the wells
above the earth: they let
the sally go (secure
keeping the end in one
hand) hands then join to swing
the bell from backstroke round
(steady!) to handstroke: arms
stretch, pull, the rope comes down
afresh with the sally
its woollen feel, handful
clasped, unclasped: resonant
with inhabited years
they will be here, these bells
for hands and hands' children
their loud dumb mouths telling
the joy of flesh to pull
(toiling, sweating) the strings
of heaven: all is not ill
when hope is in the Lord.

61

OUR HOPE IS IN THE LORD

HOPE OUR IS THE IN LORD
HOPE IS OUR IN THE LORD
IS HOPE IN OUR THE LORD
IS IN HOPE THE OUR LORD
IN IS THE HOPE OUR LORD
IN THE IS OUR HOPE LORD
THE IN OUR IS HOPE LORD
THE OUR IN HOPE IS LORD
OUR THE HOPE IN IS LORD
OUR HOPE THE IS IN LORD

HOPE OUR THE IN IS LORD
HOPE THE OUR IS IN LORD
THE HOPE IS OUR IN LORD
THE IS HOPE IN OUR LORD
IS THE IN HOPE OUR LORD
IS IN THE OUR HOPE LORD
IN IS OUR THE HOPE LORD
IN OUR IS HOPE THE LORD
OUR IN HOPE IS THE LORD
OUR HOPE IN THE IS LORD

HOPE OUR IN IS THE LORD
HOPE IN OUR THE IS LORD
IN HOPE THE OUR IS LORD
IN THE HOPE IS OUR LORD
THE IN IS HOPE OUR LORD
THE IS IN OUR HOPE LORD
IS THE OUR IN HOPE LORD
IS OUR THE HOPE IN LORD
OUR IS HOPE THE IN LORD
OUR HOPE IS IN THE LORD

62

I watch the ringers and I think of you
tall, commanding my landscape like a tower
your angelus at each appointed hour
sounding with one bell deeps beyond my due.

Come Sunday, mattins, evensong they ring:
one, two, three, four, five and the tenor go
in Rounds, they call them, and at least I know
that you have more bells than I have heard swing.

Suppose I were to climb into your chamber
conduct your ringers, bid them pull, proclaim a
Grandsire or Stedman peal: but you declare

that you have had your fill of Changes, Hunts
depend upon the hunter, so what chance
have I when you wring silence from your hair?

63

Procession

Not *piobaireachd* for they are many
and marching but Amazing Grace
with tartan bags and tasselled pipes
leads the loud progress a streetful
of feet and slow wheels lorryloads
of folk acting out their favourite
television serial Dads' Army
Emergency Task Force On The Buses
false boobs and whiskers funny hats
wobbly poses waving laughing
children cheering dogs barking
now at a silver band going oom
and of course pah as one man
thumps with knobbed sticks his chest
proud with a drum then come
civic bodies in cars and vans
Rotarians Royal British Legion
still doing their bit and after them
the entire staff of Mr Kum's restaurant
in traditional tunics and trousers
stride in a quincunx one bearing
a banner that tells you where to get
a good meal another banging
a gong and finally no less
percussive an orchestra
of oil drums playing almost a tune
everyone holding out enamel
bowls woks pudding basins chamber
pots to catch our coins for this is
Hospitals Day.

64

Incident at Eton

That afternoon a thud stopped all our hearts
rattled our windows: in these peaceful parts
it felt like war. I went out to my gate
and saw my neighbours all along the street
as though the Queen, or Christ, were due to pass:
but then another thud shook flesh and glass.
I seized my bicycle, pedalled away
towards the bridge across the motorway:
two clouds unknown to meteorologists
were drifting where each Tudor chimney twists
upward beside the Gothic pinnacles
of Eton. As I gazed, the hallowed halls
sent up a third cloud, and a third thud struck.
The Revolution had arrived, with luck!
I hastened to the scene, and in a meadow
saw lorries, heavy ordnance in whose shadow
figures in uniform moved here and there –
the college boys were those with longer hair.
I marched up to a man in a peaked cap
a baton in his armpit. 'Yes, old chap?'
I pointed to the concrete blocks of Slough:
'A hundred thousand people want to know
what's going on.' 'The school invited us:
we have cadets here.' 'But a minibus
could easily have brought the boys to you
without all these manoeuvres. Cheaper too.'
A master overheard, joined us. 'Oh dear.
We didn't tell the local papers. We're
most awfully sorry.' Back at home I rang
the police, asked if they had heard a bang.
'We've had a few inquiries. It's been warm
hasn't it? Yes, a freak electric storm.'

65

Musical Ride

All the King's horses and all the King's men
(says a gun carriage cast in a masculine reign)
emerge in their splendour as dusk turns to dark
to practise their perilous dance in our park.

In red and in gold (blood and glory) careering
they seem not to worry whose turf they are tearing
to music round flagpoles in figures of eight
to the wonder of peasants who stand round and wait.

But we are plebeians with uncles and aunts
who see a less lovable form of the dance
where orange and green are the colours that matter
when armoured cars muster and radios chatter.

At the mid hour of night they have sat in our street
rehearsing for what they were warned they would meet
and no one complained of the smell and the noise
for it could mean employment for some of our boys.

The music has stopped and the horses are sweating
and then we remember the treat we are getting
but all the King's horses and all the King's men
cannot put a province together again.

66
Holy Saturday

Walking through St Mary's churchyard
   with the washing I can hear
from the windows *Pange lingua*
   gurgling down the twilight air
as the organist rehearses
   for the high day of the year.

I have seen the sullen faces
   in the all-night launderette
dark eyes fixed upon the windows
   where the sun will never set:
though the world is turning, turning
   it will not be whiter yet.

He will ransom us tomorrow
   he whom yesterday we sold:
for the children of the promise
   silver shall be turned to gold
but today we work in darkness
   smoothing linen fold by fold.

67

Saturday Night

>   for Krysia Kocjan

The din begins. Unusual words:
'O what can ail thee, knight-at-arms . . .'
It cannot be John Keats with steel
    guitars and drums?

But listen . . . 'lily on thy brow . . .
a fading rose . . . a faery's child':
it is La Belle Dame Sans Merci
    but wild, man, wild!

I have heard Stanford do his best
and Hindemith do what he can
but now it is the daughter of
    a working man

her name foreign enough to be
a native of this town, who sings
of the young hero in the dead
    landscape and brings

a sudden lump to the throat. She takes
the poem at face value: here is
a ballad, and oblivious of
    Romantic theories

she turns it straight into a song
and sings it straight to all these folk
who do not read – could not among
    these lights, this smoke.

I have brought too much luggage here
I know, but luggage is not all
when the young woman on the stage
    has me in thrall.

68

Assumption

Fair as the moon, choice as the sun
                          Assunta
on her name day in Protestant England
where it is only a princess's birthday
has tried to do it again
instead of her family back home
doing it for her
                  Who is this
going up through the wilderness
like a column of smoke
                  Billy
has asked the porter who is a student
to correct a letter: I wish to marry
your daughter and I promise that we will
live loving to each other
                  perfumed
with myrrh and incense
                  Piggy
yawns at the switchboard: every night
he takes over from crumpet, puts
a hand down his trousers, scratches
audibly, rolling his bloodshot
eyes, reeking of gin
                  and scented
like cinnamon and balm
                  Almost
Sunday and the ambulances
are coming in like buses: Irishmen
with pouring noses, Pakistanis
new to liquor, a boy with half his face
left on the front of a lorry
                  and like
a spring day she will be surrounded
with roses
            A young woman
pants in the hot red dark, an old woman

sighs: the divine economy
                    and lilies
of the valley
            A hand over the eyes
a folding back of sleeves
                    A poured out ointment
thy name
            and up the corridor
the snick, snick of a trolley wheel, the slow
approach of the death wagon: dull zinc
topped by a rickety green canvas hood
with a small celluloid window
                        taken up
to a bed of ether
            Lift
the calico bundle – careful, lad, the neck
breaks easy with the muscles slack, slide
on, put back the hood: they need her bed –
no time to let her stiffen
                    and cassia
from thy garments, from the houses
of ivory
        Down the corridor and rattle
out across the old workhouse yard
to the little house by the gate: unlock
the door, smell
hosepipes, rubber gloves, cold
                        We run
to the smell of thy ointments
                The light
dazzles: yesterday's autopsy, covered
but for the head – gaunt face and brow
long hair combed out over the slab
white and still as a star
                    our girls
delighted too much in thee.

69

Limbo Dance

'By the rivers of Babylon', the first
psalm to make it into the Hit Parade
batters our eardrums and the bright lights burst

about us in a simulated air raid
but this time it is not a cue to dance
for people move until a space is made

and Lenny dressed in red and white silk pants
and nothing else comes on with two fine girls
who smile and wave as breasts and buttocks bounce

and they put up on pedestals two poles
six feet apart and between these they sling
having first fitted pegs in level holes

a third pole which is coated with something
which they set fire to with a flaming brand
and Lenny can begin. We form a ring

to hear the Lord's song sung in a strange land
for though we hanged our harps upon the willows
here is a concrete floor with a steel band:

old oil drums upside down and in the hollows
that were their bottoms circles have been burned
of different sizes for a scale that bellows

out of the depths, but nothing here is mourned
by this metal menagerie. By now
Lenny has danced under the flames and turned

to face the fire next time. The two girls bow
to our applause and lower by a notch
the pole beneath which Lenny's head must go

and go it does, slowly, and does not touch
the pole, and does not, cannot bow, but tips
back, and his knees bend forward as we watch

breathless. The two girls smile, wagging their hips
waving their hands. From the West Indies, rum,
tobacco, cotton, sugar in great ships

headed for England: out of England come
cloth, iron, brandy, guns to soften West
Africa. Still the steel drums bang and boom

and Lenny dares the fire to scorch his chest
but dances under. From West Africa
across to the West Indies, people, pressed

together, chained in rows, carried away
captive: cloth, iron, brandy, guns exchanged
for rum, tobacco, cotton, sugar. They

lower the pole to the last notch. All ranged
below in berths six feet by two by two
and once more those who cannot be revenged

are being redeemed as Lenny dances through
the two-foot gap left between floor and flame
flat yet unfallen, shoulders working to

and fro, arms in a mock embrace, a gleam
white in his eyes, remembering despair
his mouth wide open yet he does not scream

but comes up smiling, wipes his hands. We cheer.

70
Palmy Days

>> for Fr Sydney Hinkes

Palmy days, when the vicar preached
in the Sikh temple and his wife
>> sported a sari:
> it took the edge off life.

Before the law told us to love
our neighbour, the International
>> Friendship Council
> would put on concerts: all

the local talent (the more multi-
racial the better) would be there
>> beaming goodwill –
> an impresario's nightmare.

A Jewish family string quartet
would play (yes) 'From My Life', a Scot
>> in foreign sporran
> would dance upon one spot

the Morris men in hose and bells
would jingle, skip, wave sashes, hit
>> cudgels together
> to the whine of a kit

Lenny would bring his girls, his fire
and dance limbo to Claude's steel band
>> before white folk
> and all would understand

then the Great Britain and Ireland
Photographic Society
>> who once they were
> registered found that they

preferred music, would exercise
that louder preference and come
    to sing to a
hand-held harmonium

while a guitarist and a girl
with a sitar would do their best
    to reconcile
the sounds of East and West

and knowing there was little chance
that fugue and *rag* would fraternise
    would sigh and play
some sort of Indo-jazz.

Palmy days, when in peasant garb
the Poles would pace out their mazurkas:
    a shame we saw
so little of the workers.

71

Romney

> Oui, dans une île que l'air charge
> De vue et non de visions

Petite Jatte, Romney
this Roman Island between
shire and shire, town and country
where all conditions of men

meet this Sunday between spring
and summer to cast a hook
that speech may catch their meaning
between the weir and the lock.

The way on to the island
is across the narrow bridge
two gates form when they are joined
against the current and *Midge*

and *River Princess* go up
or down, for once together
and a smooth hand grasps a rope
and two worlds touch each other

but NO FISHING IN LOCK CUT
says a notice and we must
pass the iron and concrete
to a wooded grassy waste

where college boys in straw hats
watch men in gumboots and caps
standing rapt with cigarettes
dangling from their lower lips

as they grip their rods and chuck
fistfuls of elderberries
on the water for a mock
rainstorm that the fish may rise

and the current tugs the line
swirling from the weir downstream
and they haul back, cast again
haul, cast, movement against time

maybe speech against silence
a fistful of rhymes to raise
whatever is down there since
here most of the water flows.

'Here, dad.' One of the brighter
college boys might guess dimly
that this is no backwater
and might recall Mallarmé:

Yes, on an island perfumed
More with first than second sight
Each flower more flagrantly bloomed
Without our discussing it –

everything that is the case
('Here, dad') goes on being so
not needing or heeding us
but it is man who must go

against the current sometimes
even cross to the wild side
and try to tame it with names
from his little box. 'Here, dad':

a shrill voice insists from where
womenfolk in a man's world
check their nails and pat their hair
tinted for the trip and curled

flick dry soil off nylon slacks
crunch popcorn and hope for bass
while beside their outspread macks
music chatters in the grass.

'Lemme have a go with that
rod' – the new daughter-in-law:
she will learn, lad, but not yet
and male fingers slowly draw

from a little box aboil
with white maggots one which they
twirl to straighten, then impale.
Elderberries plip: away

flies the line, the reel buzzes
and dad hands the rod over
flattered but uneasy as
she stands up to the river.

'Sometimes he lets me take them
off the hook' she giggles. This
is one of the things (downstream
the line runs) that are the case

when on our island between
places, people, seasons, speech
and silence we shoot a line
not knowing what we shall catch:

in the reeds the family net
waits like a womb or a book
for a wriggler to fill it
between the weir and the lock.

72

A Private Person

Towards the end her mother was completely
paralysed except for one finger
pressing an electric buzzer day and night
to summon the stay-at-home unmarried daughter.

She was a darling, she mused, old herself now
dutiful as ever, still at the same address
dusting an ancient sideboard with its faded
sepia photos and souvenirs of the Raj.

An only child, she turned out to be bookish
so daddy, who was something on the railways
arranged for her to write holiday brochures
anonymously because she was a girl:

she had free travel, made such a lot of friends
who every year received a Christmas card
from the tall lady with the braided hair
the pince-nez and the passion for hard facts.

Somerset, Surrey, Wales and above all
her adopted Buckinghamshire she celebrated:
from Brittany, Sweden, Poland she returned
to write the history of her home town.

She kept her books in garden sheds because
there was no room among the ornaments
and she invited friends to plant a flower
that as she weeded she might think of them.

In middle age she married a widower
and they were briefly happy: she called him by
his bardic name, for he had twice been crowned
and left her two huge dragon-snarling thrones.

Alone again, she would invite her friends
one or two at a time so that she could
concentrate on them, to tea and home-made cake
whistling softly as she put the kettle on

and when they brought their children she would become
a child with them, asking, listening, giving,
ignoring their parents and assuring them
that she was on their side, which puzzled them.

With the years her garden paths grew narrower
vandals attacked her fences, her house was cold
and she was more and more a private person
reading *The Times*, writing her articles.

Was it her privacy she was defending
when a neighbour, missing her at church one Christmas
had to break in and found her lying propped
against her front door, indignant to the last?

73

So intimate, the poet says, reporting
a lady just back from the concert room
decrying critics who must rub the bloom:
but what about the artist who is courting?

He writes or paints, but not from me to you
only, for total strangers come and thank him
for preludes, poems, portraits which now rank him
among a gallery they keep from view.

So intimate . . . come close: the A flat Prelude
ends with a passage (if I did not tell, you'd
never know: though I do, you do not care)

pianissimo but for one low note's toll.
To me it says . . . but like the latest Pole
you shake my public sounds out of your hair.

For John Phillips [74-77]

74

In this field, on a tree stump
I stand. Around me
grass, other trees, birds, sky
a motorway for whose sake
I was felled. Not I
but this tree
tell the number of my limbs
ransom this loss.

75

Rescue, not
women of the streets, stray
dogs, children, but
root, bole, bough
bringing them home
to follow them where
they will, my chisel
going with the grain.

76

Crisis is
forked branches
with a bulge
between – two
arms held high
and a head
pierced with one
eye.

77

Promise of life, I call
these nut shapes: see the grain
turn as the womb
rounds, as the head
thrusts. Hard
but giving, heavenward
man carves a shoot, a root
down into ravaged soil.

For Philip Bergner

78

'Nature has no outline
but Imagination has'
                    Back
to Nature then, not to escape
Imagination, but the bounding
the binding line that says *is*
rather than *seems*.
                There are
other grammars, the accidence of light
falling on that mass, toning it
red and brown –
            catch it as it falls
before Adam names it *house*.
                    Light has
another tongue, that licks where
and when it will: *house* by night
is concentrated darkness
the eye goes round.
                That is the line
the boundary with chaos: there is
no other.
        My syntax
is all verbs: not *tree* but
life grows greenly up, not *river* but
life ripples and runs on.
                I do not know
how tomorrow will look.
                        Skill
is unlearning, a deliberate
unknowing of your place:
I stake out canvas, my sole
domain.
    I do not believe:
I see.

79

The light licks
two glasses on
to a tablecloth

but sets a plastic
flowerpot beside them
aflame in its tripod

a spider plant
clambering
over the rim.

80

A village of greys and blues
swept towards a sky where light
bursts through cloud, shatters
                        We talk
of your last painting, of the weather since –
a night of storm, tiles torn off roofs, sick elms
blown down, their roots with half a ton of earth
making great black mounds even in darkness, then
innocent day levelling all things
the heavy silence, the mouth dry, the eyes
too slow to read the paper
                      I recall
climbing into your loft, picking our way
among two thousand boards and canvases
you echoing Turner ('to paint what I see
not what I know is there') and attacking Munch
for his warped vision: art is normative
simplifying appearances, you say
to straighten sight
                        I used to think you prim
reducing all to radiant blues and greens
intolerant of those who probe the pain
but now I see: where others lie, you stand.

81

If you do not come
too close, rough edges
of light are a tree
are five trees upon
an island
        a hand
shaping not blocking
sky, not fixing it
but letting it turn
to water, if you
do not come too close.

82

'Moment of truth' you mutter, but words
are not your way. You sit down on the chair
opposite and stare at me
as if to say something important. Then
you wrinkle up your eyes, pulling your mouth
into a smile or sneer, but we are both
alone. The silence leans.   On an impulse
you reach out at the white space beside me:
I hear you dab and scrabble, I dare
not look. Your stare
returns to me: you take a piece
of smoky glass, peer through
at me. I want to giggle
but fear to break a spell.   Strokes become
touches, looks between them grow
longer, as in chess. You move: I glance
at my flat double looming. You said once
you did not like to impose your will
and I suggested that you preferred trees

which could not answer back. Have you made me
a tree?
  'One must know when to stop' you say
and invite me to look. What would a tree
say? It is me – the hair, the nose – but me
behind my name, known but not met. Though it
may live with me or not, I have to live
with it, and it more than a son
will outlive me. The light has shifted.
The afternoon has changed everything.

83

Light, but love too
of known places

a white wall climbing
to a chimney
in Templewood Lane

the blue shadow
of Windsor Castle

Fulmer tucked
like a bag of myrrh
between hills

the light on cooling
towers
  or greeting me
at dawn a grey road
rising through houses
the sun touching
a roof with quite
the right red.

84

                    To go on we must
drop must hand over to the force that is
in us as one who said I am the vessel
through which the *Sacre* passed but lest it over-
whelm us we must recognise its features
a river driven by nothing but its own
weight and come to that lock which cannot tame
the whole of us only a narrow stream
to carry the everyday traffic of word and deed
leaving the rest to rise to a longer course
more bright and brave but first
to plunge over this weir
tuning the great white noise to a silent sign.

85

It is your hour, a summer dawn: I write
because I cannot sleep, nor may with you.
The light is watercolour, clear, so blue
it seems to blot out memories of night.

It is your hour and I will tell you why:
from fresh start to fresh start you never learn –
a clean sheet every time, a new leaf's turn.
A swan flies past, its wingbeat like a cry.

When life is difficult you take a string
and thread upon it your old wedding ring.
How like this dawn you innocently stare

when I ask if you sport upon your breast
a trophy: oh, if you would but protest
and shake the makeshift necklace from your hair!

Cecilia Neal [86-91]
1968-1974

86

Cecilia, a Roman girl of whom
little is known except the holy part
was quietly sleeping off her martyrdom
when a loud sound awoke her with a start.

'Bless me!' she cried, forgetting where she was
for she was blest already: 'what was that?'
'That', said the good Lord patiently, 'was brass.
Now here is woodwind: clarinet, B flat.'

She listened and could not help wondering
what it was all about. 'Percussion next'
the Lord announced, 'and finally the string
family. Got it? Right. The feast is fixed.'

'What feast?' she asked. 'Why, yours', the good Lord said:
'you are the patron saint of all musicians.
The Church has just declared you qualified
and so you will be, soon. Congratulations.

'In stained glass windows you will pluck and blow
your voice will be in tune, your fingers nimble:
so down to work, my girl. Music, you know
is not all sounding brass and tinkling cymbal.'

The episode is not well documented
but whether she was musical or nay
to honour her upon the feast appointed
musicians take their instruments and play.

We may be just as certain that this child
CECILIA will have a sound upbringing.
We wish her health, and all her hopes fulfilled.
We wish her joy, and may her joy be singing.

87

I watch him as he tunes our piano:
he hits the tuning fork against his head
and holds it to his ear – middle C.
Then fifths and octaves outward, fingers
finding a string, inserting a cleft stick
to isolate it, fingers
finding the key, turning it with a handle
talking all the while
about his customers, imitating
their voices ('Ow did uw know
I'm Welsh, then?') seeing
the best in them: you've got to be
optimistic with a misty optic
he says. And his music: Tallis,
Byrd, Gibbons, his wife
transcribing them for him, his sons,
his little girl Cecilia. Like sunlight
on a church door, he says, the calm
gloom within. People ask him
what it's like: imagine, he says
a curtain of oil. Six days a week
he tunes pianos and on the seventh
he sings in the Chapel Royal –
a clear alto from such a portly frame
a rare spirit. There:
it is done. I walk him to the gate
where he will hail a lift to his next piano.
I say goodbye, turn, go. He stands and waits.

88

Throw the stone
    into
number one
    follow

overtake
    hopping
on one foot
    on two
then again
    on one
through the squares
    turn round
and hop back
    bending
to pick up
    the stone
and throw it
    into
number two
    follow
and so on
    she plays
little girl
    sparrow
two for a
    farthing
but her hairs
    numbered
as the squares
    her days.

89

The talking begins
about four this May
the lilac wan at the window
the road sign saying GIVE WAY

the waste of darkness beyond
over whose pebbles
the drift and ripple
of dumb syllables

a sleepless man worrying
paper with the point
of a pencil
silent

with the drive and wrestle
of these words
because he must
not as birds

that have to chatter
light into their world
but to plead early
for a friend's child.

Lord of mountain and molehill
reconciler
of rival claims on your time
look over here

where you are also wanted:
remember
Cecilia.
Do not number

her days yet
as you number ours:
you are reckless enough
with unimportant years

you who have declared
that you would miss
if it were struck dumb this dawn
one meaningless voice.

As day now floods this bowl
let your mercy begin:
is it really your hand
we feel helpless in?

90

'You've seen those pictures in the papers
of starving babies? That's how she looked
that night, except for the lump that seemed
to grow larger minute by minute.
I was all alone with her. By dawn
she was very poorly: I ran out
to get a nurse. Seconds or was it
hours later I came back and she breathed
out, hard, once
full in my face. I was just in time.'

91

Up the church path the small procession winds.
Let's see who's died this week, you used to say:
that were a little 'un – pointing. The priest leads
into the church. A trolley with a box
no bigger than a pram.
                      An angel of God
                      I have for a lover
                      who with too much zeal
                      guards my body
You did not know what was happening. How could you?
We with all our dark years knew its name
but that was no help to anyone.
                              Bright creature
whose last words were about what you liked to eat
and how long you had worn your socks, we speak now
in words beyond you, to you, for we must.

What a strange year it must have been
your sixth and last: a year of hands –
your mother's, lingering, probing in the bath
the beginning of it all, your father's
reading you like a score and questioning
the Master's ear, the doctors' hands

cool as their instruments, the kindly healer's
over you like a sunbeam, saying
he could feel warmth, something
going away .
                and the grown-ups then
puzzling you with their tears! A miracle
they called it, the X-ray plate
clear, the doctors shaking their heads and saying
It doesn't add up, your mother wondering how
to thank the healer, knitting him a sweater
because it was also a work of hands.

                      She tamed her limbs
the book says, but no hands could hold
this riot of the flesh that swung
elsewhere: meanwhile
the machines, the medicines which made you
sick in the mornings like a pregnant lady
had thinned your blood until it was no match
for the kindlier pneumonia.

Coming out of the church
                while organs sang
              she chanted in her heart
              to the Lord only
                        we hear
loud music the organist asked
permission to play, we smell
damp leaves, an early mist
over the river meadows: Autumn
we would have said to you.
                    What can we say
when we are blurred and waiting for the wind
because of you, because of you?

If you have wisdom now, perhaps you know
we speak for the dead that the living may overhear
perhaps you know these are for your mother

your father, your two tall brothers
to touch, to help them mourn, to turn
in the wind of their grief, calling your name.

Grant rest, untender Lord who give
and take away, to this small shade
CECILIA
       your handmaid who served you
       like a bee
              our sweetness
who had just begun to follow her saint
who loved to play hopscotch, to dance
down the brief springtime of her days.

92

Resurrection

Are you there?
    Who's that?
      Is it
you, honey child?
     I am flowers – oak, broom
meadowsweet. Call me Blodeuwedd, Flowerface
but I am grass too, grown so high
I cover my name.
     It's been a long time.
         Bells
bells.
  I pulled the tenor for the Diamond
Jubilee, from village to village
walking from tower to tower, a great
peal.
   I heard it in the fields.
       The factories
called me out of the mines.
       Out of the mills
me.
  My sober wishes never learn'd
to stray. Out of Egypt have I called
my son.
    We've got a Nazarene here, lads!
Singing, you never heard such singing.
And the preacher!
     Pegleg got up
fell flat on his face.
     Vanity.
      Voices
wisps of air.
    They comfort me.
       Music

heard through the womb wall: the child
quickens.
              As the sun that shines through glass
so Jesus in his Moder was.
                        A world
of light.
        Stars, stars.
                    I saw further
than any man, found a new planet.
I laid my telescope across the lawn
and Come (said the King) my Lord Archbishop
(taking his hand) I will show you the way
to heaven.
          I was a bishop
who talked of heaven with my godless, rich
neighbour: his window winks at evensong
his cross is grander far than mine. Here
we wait side by side.
                    I was a pillar
of the community, a builder who raised
a fine stone to my wife. Under her name
I had my own cut, with my trade
that all should see.
                   I was no man's wife
but subject only to the true
King. I dared to be just (see where it says!)
in the reign of George the Second.
                                  I killed my wife
after looking at her for thirty years.
We outlived Latvia to end the tale
in our front parlour.
                    I was born here
with a tumour my mother found
when she was bathing me. How old am I
now?
      I am dust blown from a chimney. I worked
to give my children a better life. I play
only now.

                I bore many children
one of whom alone had the misfortune
to survive me. He has written it
here.
            My words, mindful of th' unhonour'd dead
are well known but too few. My verses are
a narrow cell.
                My narrow cell
suits me well: I won the Cambridgeshire
the Ascot Cup the Alexandra Plate
the Gold Vase the Ascot Stakes
the Prince of Wales Stakes the Derby the Oaks
the Two Thousand the One Thousand Guineas.
Read: 'Tis the pace that kills.
                                    I fell
at Ladysmith.
            At Wipers.
                            At Omaha
Beach.
        Where's that?
                            A distant shore.
                                        Where's that
from?
    Mmm.
                Aaa.
                        My heart is sinking
I said. Only fifteen I was.
                            We saw
the veins swelling.
                    The wind lifts leaves.
                                            Ooo.
Listen!
        Children are walking, are running
over us!
            Out of us!
                        Playing!
                                Is it their mothers

or the angel calling?
                Ohoo!
                        Oh
who?
    GLORIA!
    BLODWEN!
    GEORGE!
    MARIA!
    WILLIAM!
    JAMES!
    PHILIP!
    SOPHIA!
    HENRY!
    SARAH!
    GUNNAR!
    CECILIA!
    DOROTHY!
    THOMAS!
    HARWANT!
    ARNOLD!

93

All Saints: the Poles, the Irish come and go
tending their dead, each grave a little garden
where lily and carnation ease the burden
of faces lost, and let corruption grow.

Meanwhile I who am no believer pace
the narrow path of slight acquaintance, clip
a blade of grass, tidy a marble chip
in honour of a dream, not of a face.

They celebrate what was, but I am he
who took precautions against what might be:
now haunted by what never was, I dare

summon you to my sterile festival
that I at least may lay a ghost that still
twitches a vain petition from its hair.

94

Sunnymeads

someret syäntä vasten

   Dawn sun strained through mist
white lake white islands white bridge
   one moorhen swimming

its dot of a head nodding
purposefully back and forth

   its body making
silent rings in the water
   disturbing the world

unaware of being watched
or it would scuttle away

   to hide among reeds
to forget brave purposes
   to bob up and down

till the ripples die away
and the reflections return

   is the world disturbed
more by advance than retreat
   the bird does not care

dabbling between life and death
watchful only for itself

   the rings and ripples
the difference between eating
   and being eaten

the reflections neither here
nor there in a solid world

    but man who watches
in this interval between
    acts connects it all

he makes worlds with his knowledge
and will not be forgiven

    he knows that this lake
is a disused gravel pit
    beautiful by chance

he recalls an ancient verse
'the gravel against the heart'

    his mind is driven
like the moorhen's nodding head
    across the water

but now the nod means yes yes
as his little son said once

    miaow moo baa woof woof
that is how they all say yes
    those were happy days

when yes was a nod to life
and whiteness was innocence

    making a new start
settling in this country place
    where they knew no one

no man's land where four shires meet
but do not greet each other

    now they know people
but the boundaries have moved
    and greetings are vain

at this deserted station
lost among water meadows

   near Milton's village
famous for the nightingale
   that warbl'st at eeve

far from Towers and Battlements
boosom'd high in tufted Trees

   the heart's four chambers
Buckinghamshire Middlesex
   Surrey and Berkshire

under an airport flight path
the threat of a motorway

   not worth stopping for
and yet they stopped and took on
   present and future

not knowing the heart could stop
and its four chambers foreclose

   the confident child
runs down avenues of air
   watching his body

not the rapt contemplation
of a reflected likeness

   arms and trunk and legs
himself carrying himself
   out into knowledge

away from this gravel pit
to which his father returns

    to ask what went wrong
as though a moorhen could say
    anything but yes

when he knows that innocence
is no more than ignorance

    the man tries to find
his way parting the whiteness
    of his ignorance

to arrive perhaps by noon
at the darkness of knowledge

    where there is neither
forgiving nor forgiveness
    but acknowledgement

a man may learn what he is
what he was what he can be

    whether for her sake
who shared becoming with him
    or for his own sake

the gravel against the heart
may be no more than ballast

    in this country place
where besides a lake there are
    islands and a bridge

and a moorhen's head nodding
unaware of what it does.

95

Encounter

Maybe something you have said
about wanting a child
when you see unmarried friends
producing, a leftover
from slavery, but for you
a matter of sexual
politics
        inflames me
when snow is on the ground
and ice on the heart
                      I glare
like winter sunlight
from an unfamiliar
angle
       'What is it like
to be lusted after?'
                      no way
for a friend to behave –
mauling, feeling the blood
ache back
            but you smile
declining the compliment
of my hand which beside yours
looks so bloodless
                      and we talk
of ancestral villainy
and I praise your person
because I still hope, then
I praise your style, enjoying
my male paradox until
I see your lower lip
trembling
                Thank you
for taking me in your stride.

96

The White Peacock

A damp, forgotten village by the Thames:
knowing that you had lived there long years since
I went that afternoon to pick up hints
looking at cottages and reading names.

Knowing that you had lived there long years since
I hoped to hear some echo of my dreams
looking at cottages and reading names
for on my life you left your fingerprints.

I hoped to hear some echo of my dreams
in pub, in shop, where people looked askance
for on my life you left your fingerprints.
The church was locked. I tramped among the tombs:

in pub, in shop, where people looked askance
I ventured also but received no welcomes.
The church was locked. I tramped among the tombs
then through a wicket gate set in the fence

I ventured also but received no welcomes
pausing because the greenery was dense:
then through a wicket gate set in the fence
I came upon a garden full of blooms.

Pausing because the greenery was dense
and on the property I had no claims
I came upon a garden full of blooms
where a white peacock did its slow, stiff dance.

And on the property I had no claims
so, turning on my heel, I wandered thence
where a white peacock did its slow, stiff dance:
my aspirations grounded, lost my aims.

97

The Elderberry Tree

>   in memory of Barbara Cox

With its thick stems and tangled twigs
growing by this disused canal
it looks like a giant weed, but twice in summer
it will yield sweetness to the tongue.

In high July it opens to the sun
handfuls of delicate white blossom –
a bride weighed down with promises:
take her by day and she will fill
your house with fragrance, and your jars
with light cool wine to quench your noontide thirst.

As summer lengthens towards Michaelmas
if you have spared some blossom
her berries ripen, white has turned
to a purple so deep it seems to throb –
each cluster a breast, the green stalks
so many veins flushing to feed their tips
all yours to gather: you climb, take hold of boughs
bending them to your will until your cup is full.

But I left it too late this year: Michaelmas
came and went as I waited for just
a little more sun, but October brought the cold
and when I went out for my berries
I saw not shrivelled globes, nor yet bare twigs
stripped by another's hands, but the green stalks
intact, pecked empty by the hungry birds.

98

Tracks

From the edge of the Moat
a track north-east
for half a mile

from the edge of the Mound
a track south-east
for a third of a mile

meeting at right angles
in the Grove at a point
midway between
King's Cottage and Queen's Cottage

in the village where
every Whitsun they buried
the likeness of a beast

in the village where
in happier days we lived
and our son grew up.

Old men's tales at most
but between Moat and Mound
in the crook of each other's arms
we were King and Queen.

Go there now and you will find
a scrapyard where an alsatian
tries to bite off your hand.

99

Quand vous serez bien vieille

When you are old and lost in memory
you might, seized by a sentimental fit
take down this book and blow the dust off it
recalling: 'Bosley was quite keen on me.'

Your husband, nodding opposite, would start:
'Eh, what was that?' You would repeat the name.
'That poet.' 'No, I don't remember him.
But you were always stealing someone's heart.'

I shall be dust by then and out of print
who pestered you and could not take a hint
that you preferred another man, ma chère

who would not sell his birthright for a yes
from you, and was not driven by distress
to seek in you what simply was not there.

100

Moving Indoors

It is time to move indoors, to gather up
papers and books and cigarettes and beer
and balancing them all in one hand, grip
the doorknob with the other, push the door
open, put down my load and once more step
outside and try to fold up the deckchair
a little damp by now: sitting here once
I turned my heartbeats into one brief dance.

'You are bringing my house down': I was proud
of that, its bright echoes of music-hall
setting off many darker thoughts I had
of walking out on home life, work and all
responsibilities for one loud need
and I was ready with an answering call –
but it is time to move indoors, and I
gather up my frustrations with a sigh.

It may be just as well the house still stands
after the storm, after the holiday
the table in the square, the wild romance
that might have been had she not gone away
for far too much was staked upon the chance
that we would live to see another day
without the decor and beyond the Alps
where, all being equal, every little helps.

I tread once more these tidy northern streets
and window after window shows a room
where a girl plays an instrument or meets
her lover, or a lady is at home –

for it is time to move indoors, where fates
are more securely sealed: so is my doom
who courted Titian but who find Vermeer
easier to live with in this cooler air.

So much to do this autumn! Where to start?
It will be difficult to fit it in:
who are together now, who are apart
who has a show, a concert, where and when –
and as a film of ice forms on the heart
left out by accident we learn again
to close the windows and to hear the hours
tick by, for it is time to move indoors.

Notes

Hundred: 'ten times ten . . . a subdivision of a county or shire, having its own court' (OED). The Chiltern Hundreds were the three subdivisions of South Bucks – from west to east, Desborough, Burnham, Stoke. This last, named after Stoke Poges, is today shared with Berkshire and dominated by the urban sprawl of Slough. A useful companion during the long making of this book has been *The History of Slough* by Maxwell Fraser, MA, FRHistS (Slough 1973), who would not have approved my occasional use of gossip as a source. She is commemorated in the dedication and in poem 72.

Poem **1**. *Ivy-mantled Tow'r*: Upton is the more likely setting of Gray's *Elegy* than Stoke Poges, where the poet's mother lived and where they are buried.

Arago: François Arago (1786-1853), French astronomer and physicist.

Poem **7**. Alfred A. Wolmark (1877-1961), Polish-Jewish artist who settled in London. See Pevsner, *The Buildings of England: Buckinghamshire*, and the *Jewish Chronicle Colour Magazine* of 21 May 1976.

Poem **9**. See Felix Aylmer, *Dickens Incognito* (London 1969).

Poem **18**. See *Finnegans Wake*, end of Part I.

Poem **29**. Inquiries after the sculptor have so far drawn a blank.

Poem **36**. *Signor mio car*: from a sonnet of Michelangelo.

Poem **38**. *Lata*: Lata Mangeshkar, Indian popular singer.

Poem **44**. *The Old Woman of Beare*: 'one of the standard revenant figures of early Irish literature' (Frank O'Connor). See his anthology *Kings, Lords, and Commons*.

Poem **50**. *Smrt*: Serbo-Croat 'death'.

Poem **51**. A few details may not tally with official accounts, but the speaker was there.

Poem **55**. Echoing 'Lead us, heavenly Father, lead us', a popular hymn at weddings.

Poem **57**. The hymn quoted is by Charles Wesley, *The English Hymnal* No. 303, where the tune bears its English name Lovely.

Poem **58** is indebted to Laurence Binyon, Jon Silkin, Wilfred Owen and Geoffrey Hill.

Poem **59**. See Dorothy L. Sayers' thriller.

Pamela: her novel by Samuel Richardson.

OUR HOPE IS IN THE LORD: inscription on a bell at Langley Marish.

Poem **60**. The vowel *e* is 'hunted' like the treble (smallest bell) in Plain Bob Minor, a peal on six bells.

Poem **61**. A transcription of Grandsire Doubles, whereby changes are rung on five bells with the tenor (largest bell) bringing up the rear. All very elementary to ringers, but apparently new to poetry.

Poem **63**. *Piobaireachd*: pibroch, the traditional 'piping' of one player.

Poem **67**. Some time in the 1970s Krysia Kocjan (formerly of Milngavie) recorded her memorable setting of Keats's poem. Though she did not sing it in any Chiltern hundred, her Polish name qualifies her as an honorary citizen.

Poem **68**. Quoting the Roman Office for the Feast of the Assumption, which quotes *The Song of Songs*.

Poem **71**. Quoting Mallarmé, *Prose pour Des Esseintes*.

Poem **78**. Quoting Blake and Turner.

Poem **81**. Quoting Eliot, *East Coker*.

Poem **83**. Recalling *The Song of Songs*.

Poem **84**. Quoting Stravinsky and Vaughan.

Poem **91**. Quoting the Office for the Feast of St Cecilia.

Poem **92**. Recalling (among others) the *Mabinogion*, a Middle English lyric, Vaughan, Herschel, local gravestones, Gray, Eliot.

Poem **94**. *Someret syäntä vasten* ('the gravel against the heart') is from a Finnish folk poem about Jesus's death and burial. Other references are to Milton's early poems, written when he stayed with his parents at nearby Horton.

Poem **99**. In the convention used by Ronsard.